FORMULA 1
MOTOR RACING BOOK

PREFACE BY FLAVIO BRIATORE & FRANK WILLIAMS

DK

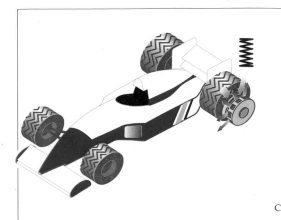

DK

A DK PUBLISHING BOOK

Commissioned and conceived by RENAULT COMMUNICATIONS
Designed and illustrated by DORLING KINDERSLEY LTD.
Written by XAVIER CHIMITS AND FRANÇOIS GRANET
Editorial coordination by PATRICK GROS

Project Directors: Bob Gordon and Helen Parker, Page Ltd.
Art Director: Peter Luff
Picture research: Julia Harris-Voss
US Editor: Jill Hamilton
Translation: Chris Williams
Special photography: Matthew Ward, Wake-Upp Productions
Illustrations: Mark Tattam, Anthony Duke, Stephen Pearce, Andrew Milne,
Models: Mark Jamieson

SPECIAL THANKS TO
Frank Dernie, Gérard Camilli, Emmanuel Collard, David Owen,
John Postlethwaite, Jessica Salisbury, Philippe Tardivel, Carbone Industrie, Elf, FIA,
I.B.S.V., Williams, Benetton and Renault Sport

Some of the technical details in this book were taken from
Conduite en compétition, byPierre-François Rousselot and Alain Prost,
Editions Robert Laffont.

PICTURE CREDITS:
Allsport: Pascal Rondeau 4 & 59, 13, 15, 17, 29, 33, 39, 40, 41, 42, 43, 46, 47; Mike Hewit
42; jacket, 13, 20, 22, 29, 33, 40, 42, 54, 56, 57, 60; Automedia 6; Autopresse News 49, 56,
57; Autosport Photographic 28, 29, 48; Bernard Asset front end, 4, 41; Philippe de Barsy
E.P.E. 56-57; DPPI 4, 5, 8, 11, 13, 14, 17, 21, 24, 28, 29, 38, 39, 41, 48, 55, 57, 61, 63, back
end; L.A.T. Photographic 8, 14, 15, 28-29, 30, 38, 39, 49, 57, 58, 63; Mary Evans Picture
Library 16; The National Motor Museum, Beaulieu 12, 15, 57, 58, 59; Sporting Pictures
(UK) Ltd 9, 11, 13, 15, 28, 29, 30, 32, 62; R.W. Schlegelmilch 25, 30; © Wake-Upp
Productions/Gérard Planchenault, Bruno des Gayets, Olivier Marguerat 1, 8, 9, 12, 15,
16, 17, 18, 18-19, 19, 21, 26, 27, 28, 29, 32, 33, 36, 37, 40, 41, 43, 44-45, 45, 46, 48, 52-53, 58-
59, 62, 64, back jacket; ZOOM/ICN 5, 11

Additional photography: Zul Mukhida, Guy Ryecart,
Dave King, Steve Swope, Peter Tempest

First American edition, 1996
2 4 6 8 10 9 7 5 3 1

Published in the United States by DK Publishing, Inc., 95 Madison Avenue,
New York, NY 10016

A catalog record is available from the Library of Congress.

ISBN 0-7894-0440-0

Color separations by Colourscan, Singapore
Printed and bound in Italy by New Interlitho, Milan.

Contents

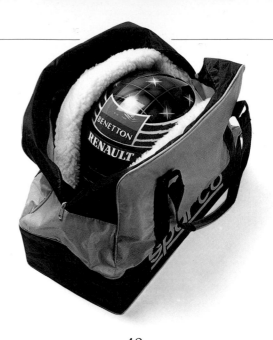

Preface

My bookshelves are literally buckling under all the books I possess on the subject of Formula 1. Yet if I were to keep just one, it would most certainly be the Renault Formula 1 Motor Racing Book. For this work – which has dissected Grand Prix racing into precise, simple words – has enabled even me to rediscover my sport. Page after page, it offers the reader a rare insight into the world that has become my daily way of life. Never before has such an informed and detailed study of how a racing team operates been undertaken.

Indeed, isn't that one of Formula 1's paradoxes? Despite being the planet's most widely followed sporting championship, what goes on away from the circuits is so often veiled in secrecy. Fleeing the limelight has practically become the golden rule.

This book, however, provides a unique opportunity to see what really goes on behind the scenes. It takes the reader into the workshops, explains the parameters engineers must work within, accompanies drivers in their race preparation, and analyzes the long chain of skills required to take a driver and his team to the very top. More than a guided tour, this album is a valuable reference document for the Formula 1 expert and newcomer alike. My only wish is that it will lead its readers to share my passion for the sport even more.

FLAVIO BRIATORE

For the motor sport fan who watches a Grand Prix on television, the excitement and pressure lasts about 90 minutes. However, for the teams, Formula 1 motor racing is a continuous race against time as we move around the world from circuit to circuit.

Whether testing or preparing cars at the factory, it is a nonstop race against the clock. For the drawing office and research and design team, it is a relentless endeavor to push back the frontiers of technology. It is also a continual combat to reduce the chance factor to its strictest minimum.

It is these aspects of motor racing that I have lived and breathed since I founded my first team at the age of 22. Yet so little is known about the sport, other than what we read in our newspapers or see on our TV screens. It is a complex business, involving hundreds of people in the case of Williams Grand Prix. It is a business that is far less spectacular than two drivers out-braking each other into a corner on a Grand Prix circuit. The Renault Formula 1 Motor Racing Book *is an impressive work which successfully bridges this gap by revealing what goes on behind the scenes in Grand Prix racing, presenting facts that the broadcasting companies and press rarely tackle.*

Everyone will learn something from this book – it is a journey into the very heart of Formula 1.

FRANK WILLIAMS

A Formula 1 car is born

THE BIRTH OF A FORMULA 1 CAR is a long and complex affair. Six to ten months are required from initial sketches to first track tests. Computers play a key role in this process. Their processing capacity and simulation software allow engineers to evaluate a car's potential. However, in the ultramodern factories of Williams and Benetton, who produce in-house some 90% of the parts they use, machines have not yet replaced human skills entirely. There is still no robot able to shape exhaust pipes that will hug the contours of the engine.

SIMULATED SPEED
Before a car is built, scale models are tested in a wind tunnel. Winds of up to 300 kilometers per hour simulate the sort of speeds the car will reach on the track.

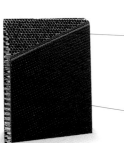

Aluminum honeycomb

Carbon sheet

CARBON SANDWICH
To build the tub, composite materials specialists bond an aluminum honeycomb between two sheets of carbon. This is then polymerized in a vacuum oven. The result is twice as light and twice as strong as ordinary aluminum.

Nomex honeycomb is even lighter than its aluminum equivalent.

NOMEX HONEYCOMB
Nomex honeycomb is used for the narrower parts of the tub such as the nose cone. While not quite as rigid as aluminum, it is lighter, more flexible, and easier to work.

HEAD OF COMPOSITE DEPARTMENT
Philip Henderson is responsible for the running of the composite department and keeping up with all the latest technology in the composite field.

MECHANIC
Max Fluckiger is No. 1 mechanic on Michael Schumacher's racing car.

RACE ENGINEER
Christian Silk is part of a group responsible for the engineering of the cars at the circuit.

DESIGN OFFICE MANAGER
Graham Heard is responsible for the organization of the Design Office.

The drawing offices and workshops of F1 teams are as well guarded as banks. Premises are jealously fenced, patrolled by security personnel, and brightly lit at night to ensure that the secrets within are kept safe.

SIX STAGES IN THE BUILDING OF A FORMULA 1 CAR

STAGE 1
Before being painted, the tub, which is made from laminated carbon sheets, is baked in a vacuum oven.

STAGE 2
The engine is rigidly mounted to the rear of the tub

STAGE 3
Side pods on either side of the tub house the radiators that cool the engine.

STAGE 4
The transmission, once it is assembled (20 hours' work), is coupled to the engine.

STAGE 5
Wishbones, suspension, brakes, and rear running gear are added.

STAGE 6
The wings, bodywork, and wheels are fitted. The car is finally mobile. Only the electronic management of the transmission and engine remains to be programmed before the car is ready to drive.

MACHINE SHOP SUPERVISOR
Kevin Young assists in the day-to-day running of the machine shop.

ELECTRONICS ENGINEER
Wayne Bennett is responsible for downloading all the data from the racing car.

PAINTWORK AND DECORATION
Tim Baston is responsible for the bodywork of the car and application of decals to those places agreed with sponsors.

MASTERMINDS OF PERFORMANCE

Among them, these nine men represent all of the different trades involved in creating a Formula 1 car. Highly qualified engineers and technicians work under the orders of the team's technical director, who can be described as the true "father" of the car. The increasing use of complex technology has led teams to recruit their engineers directly from leading technical and aeronautical universities.

AERODYNAMICS ENGINEER
James Allison is part of a team responsible for the aerodynamic development of the car.

TECHNICAL DIRECTOR
Ross Brawn has overall responsibility for design, development, and engineering of the car.

Rules and regulations

Sɪɴᴄᴇ ɪᴛꜱ ᴄʀᴇᴀᴛɪᴏɴ ɪɴ 1950, the World Championship has undergone numerous regulation changes. For reasons of safety, the governing body has periodically sought to channel the ingenuity of engineers, whose prime objective is always to improve the performance of their machine. In just over 20 pages, the championship's technical regulations clearly set out the limits within which engineers can work. A quick read reveals that a Formula 1 car is defined as "a vehicle running on at least four nonaligned complete wheels, of which at least two are for steering and at least two for propulsion." Since the designers will go to any length in order to gain those all-important hundredths of a second, this basic definition is extremely necessary.

SAFETY FUEL TANK
Fuel tanks must be deformable and puncture-proof. The "bladders" are made from rubber reinforced with Kevlar, and fuel pipes from the tank must be the automatic cutoff type.

REMOVABLE STEERING WHEEL
In order to allow drivers to climb swiftly out of the cockpit, steering wheels must be fitted with a quick-release system.

NOSE CONE
The distance between the front of the car and the centerline of the front axle may not exceed 120 cm. Width is restricted to 140 cm.

DUAL-CIRCUIT BRAKES
The braking system is divided into two independent circuits. In the event of a problem with one, the other continues to function.

IMPACT-ABSORBING BODY
Like road cars, an example of every new Formula 1 car is subjected to a crash test.

SLIM-LINE
The minimum authorized weight of a Formula 1 car – driver included – is 595 kg. There is no length restriction, but maximum values have been set for front and rear overhang. Width must not exceed 200 cm and overall height can be no more than 95 cm, measured from the lowest part of the chassis.

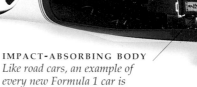

SEAT AND FULL-HARNESS BELTS
Six-point harness belts are mandatory and must be approved by the FIA.

EXPLOITING THE REGULATIONS

F1 is an ongoing combat between legislators and engineers, the former seeking to curb the creative instinct of the latter. Indeed, the task of the sport's governing body is to ensure that F1 cars stay within reasonable limits. For example, airfoil brakes (1968), the use of 6-wheels (1976), and "fan-cars" (1978) were all outlawed. Had they not been, safety might have taken a step backward while spectator interest would have gained nothing.

Tyrrell P34
6-wheeler (1976)

Rear of the Brabham
BT 46 B "fan-car"
(1978)

THE LEGISLATORS

The fourteen members of the Technical Commission are elected by the World Council, the highest authority of the Fédération Internationale de l'Automobile (FIA). These highly qualified technicians and engineers, one of whom represents the teams, prepare the regulations, which are subsequently submitted to the World Council for approval.

President

Constructors' representative

THE FIA TECHNICAL COMMISSION

FROM PREHISTORY TO THE NUCLEAR AGE

It was about ten years ago that Formula 1 teams began to turn to the aeronautical industry, rather than the automobile industry, for the recruitment of staff and to test new materials such as carbon, Kevlar, and high-performance metals and alloys, which are now commonplace.

THE 1950s
With front-mounted engines, chassis rails, "cigar" aerodynamics, narrow wheels, and drivers sitting in the upright position, the cars created in Formula 1's heroic days were similar in design to prewar cars.

A MAXIMUM OF 12 CYLINDERS
Engine capacity is restricted to 3,000cc and the number of cylinders is limited to 12. Turbocharging is not permitted and only reciprocating piston-engines are allowed, a clause which effectively outlaws rotary technology.

FOUR WHEELS
A Formula 1 car must have four wheels, the width of which may not exceed 15 in (38 cm). Bodywork must not cover the wheels.

REAR WINGS
Rear overhang must not be more than 50 cm. Wing width is limited to 100 cm while their height may not exceed 80 cm.

THE 1960s
Drivers started wearing helmets and fireproof overalls and adopted a more reclined position. Engines moved to the rear and the monocoque chassis was introduced. F1 had entered the modern era. For safety reasons, minimum weight was raised first to 450 kg, then to 500 kg.

INCONSPICUOUS SUSPENSION
Chrome-plating of suspension wishbones and pull-rods is not permitted.

TRANSMISSION
A minimum of 4 forward speeds and a maximum of 7. Reverse gear is mandatory.

THE 1970s
As radiators moved from the front to the sides, Formula 1 cars took on a more wedgelike shape. Wings, which had already begun to appear toward the end of the 60s, were inverted airplane wings fitted to improve the car's downforce.

A normally aspirated Formula 1 car: 700 bhp, 595 kg (including driver)

THE 1980s
Ground effect was restricted while skirts, aimed at creating a low-pressure zone under the cars, were outlawed in the early 80s. To increase the speed of their cars, teams turned to other means, notably turbo engines that were capable of power outputs of up to 1,200 bhp.

COMPARED WITH THE US
F1 and Indy are the world's two fastest forms of single-seater motor racing. Because of the speeds reached on America's oval circuits, Indy cars are heavier and feature a profiled undertray to keep them "glued" to the track. F1 cars tend to be more agile and sophisticated than Indy cars, as well as quicker around traditional circuits. But it would be dangerous to let an F1 car race on oval tracks.

A turbocharged Indy car: 800 bhp, 750 kg

THE 1990s

Normally aspirated 3.5-liter engine

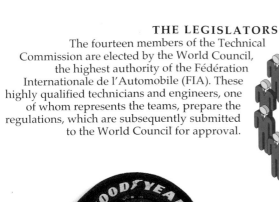

Formula 1 teams

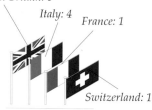

In the history of F1 not a season passes without the departure of at least one team. Invariably, their place is snapped up immediately. Since 1950, no less than 97 teams have tried their hand in F1. Only 12 were present throughout the 1995 championship, which means that 85 have disappeared over the years. In Formula 1, simply surviving is a victory in itself. The Brabham team, World Champion in 1983, disappeared less than ten years after winning its last world title. Meanwhile, Frank Williams has still not forgotten the dark days of the 1970s, when he was forced to sell all his personal effects to pay his staff. Sponsorship money tends to go to the best equipped teams, and the increase in the funds required to start a team has, over the past decade or so, resulted in a marked rise in professionalism. It is therefore increasingly difficult for a newcomer to make it to the very top. Since 1988, just four teams have tasted Grand Prix success: Williams, Benetton, McLaren, and Ferrari.

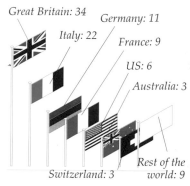

NATIONALITIES OF F1 TEAMS

Great Britain: 34
Germany: 11
Italy: 22
France: 9
US: 6
Australia: 3
Switzerland: 3
Rest of the world: 9

1950–1995

Great Britain: 6
Italy: 4
France: 1
Switzerland: 1

1995

BRITISH OR ITALIAN

Half the teams to have taken part in the championship since its creation in 1950 – and practically the entire grid in 1995 – were either British or Italian. These nationalities have tended to dominate Formula 1. No other has won a Grand Prix since 1983 (Renault) and none has taken a driver to the Drivers' crown since 1955 (Mercedes).

FORMULA 1 DEBUT

Ferrari: 1950
McLaren: 1966
Williams: 1975
Arrows: 1978
Minardi: 1985
Sauber: 1993
Tyrrell: 1970
Ligier: 1976
Benetton: 1986
Jordan: 1991
Pacific: 1994
Forti: 1995

1950
1960
1970
1980
1990

REJUVENATION

The arrival of new teams is an ongoing progress in Formula 1. Less than half the teams on the grid in 1995 had been operating for more than ten years. Benetton, created in 1986 from the former Toleman team, is the newest outfit to have tasted Grand Prix success.

COATS OF ARMS

All F1 teams have their own logos. Some, however, are more famous than others: Ferrari's prancing horse used to be the personal arms of an Italian pilot shot down during World War I. For Enzo Ferrari, a friend of the man's parents, it was a way of paying tribute to him. As for the four interlaced letters representing the initials of Anthony Colin Bruce Chapman, the founder of Lotus, these can be seen today on the nose cones of the Pacifics, following the sale of the Lotus name.

TWELVE TEAMS

A sign of the times and a consequence of the current economic climate is the fact that the number of teams in F1 has fallen consistently since 1989. That year, 20 teams took part in the World Championship. At the start of 1995, the figure had dropped to 13 and then to 12 when Simtek threw in the towel a few months into the 1995 season.

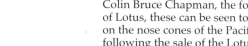

MINARDI
172 Grands Prix

TYRRELL
369 Grands Prix, 23 wins, 2 titles

FORTI
17 Grands Prix

PACIFIC
22 Grands Prix

ARROWS
272 Grands Prix

LIGIER
310 Grands Prix, 8 wins

Arrows
Jordan
Mercedes
Hart
Pacific
Yamaha
Mugen Honda
Benetton
Williams
Tyrrell
McLaren
Ford
Peugeot Sport
Renault Sport
Ligier
Sauber
Minardi
Forti
Ferrari

FORMULA 1's "SILICON VALLEY"

Oxfordshire, in the heart of England, has become the "Silicon Valley" of Formula 1. If the majority of today's teams are located within a 50-km radius of Silverstone, it is because the region boasts a high number of specialized subcontractors and skilled personnel – the result of a long local motorsport tradition. Of the 12 teams racing in Formula 1 in 1995, only four – Ligier, Sauber, Minardi, and Forti – did not have their chassis either designed or built in England.

BRUCE McLAREN

Like Jack Brabham, his teammate of the day at Cooper, McLaren was more an engineer than a driver. At the age of 28 he raced the first ever McLaren and, in 1968, he won a Grand Prix driving a car bearing his own name. It proved to be his last F1 win. On June 2, 1970, Bruce McLaren was killed at Goodwood. A quarter of a century on, McLaren cars continue to enjoy success.

FRANK WILLIAMS

A former driver himself, Frank Williams had started a number of F1 teams before founding Williams Grand Prix Engineering Ltd. in 1977. Short of funds, the company went through a number of difficult periods before finally winning its first Grand Prix with Clay Regazzoni in 1979 and its first world title in 1980 with Alan Jones. Since then, Williams' name has always figured at the forefront of the sport.

ENZO FERRARI

Ferrari is the only team that has been present in F1 since the creation of the World Championship in 1950. Right up until his death at the age of 90, Enzo Ferrari, patriarchal founder of the team, still held a firm rein on the "Scuderia." He had created a team in his own image: enchanting yet complicated. Today, it is Fiat who pulls the strings. But deep down, Ferrari hasn't changed.

SAUBER
48 Grands Prix

McLAREN
427 Grands Prix, 104 wins, 9 titles

JORDAN
81 Grands Prix

FERRARI
554 Grands Prix, 105 wins, 9 titles

WILLIAMS
346 Grands Prix, 83 wins, 5 titles

BENETTON
161 Grands Prix, 26 wins, 2 titles

Formula 1 engines

Every year since 1950, a world title has been awarded to the best driver and since 1958 another has been awarded to the best team. Officially, no championship exists for engines. However, in the public's mind, it is clearly Benetton and Renault who took the world crown in 1995, just as Williams and Renault did in 1994, 1993 and 1992. This shared perception is thoroughly justified, for in today's Formula 1 the role of the engine is equal to that played by the chassis. Honda eloquently illustrated this by becoming World Champions with Williams in 1987, and then with McLaren in 1988, having switched teams during the winter break.

154 VICTORIES!
The Ford Cosworth DFV V8 is the most successful engine in F1's history. Between 1967 and 1982, it powered practically every car on the grid, to take 154 Grand Prix wins and 10 World Championship titles.

The combustion chambers of Renault's V10 engine undergo wind-tunnel testing to identify the optimum design for efficient flow.

The carbon air box that feeds the engine's air-injection system is located above the driver's head.

The air timing system of the Renault V10 has four valves per cylinder.

The fuel injection ramp of the Renault V10 is hewn out of solid metal.

Titanium bolts are used to mount the clutch housing to the engine.

RENAULT F1

Camshafts are now gear-driven. Those of the 1989 RS1 Renault V10 were belt-driven.

Air timing has removed the need for valve springs. Valves are now driven by compressed air.

Dry-sump lubrication involves pumping oil into the sump under pressure. Scavenger pumps then pick up the oil and dispatch it to a tank located inside the transmission housing.

RENAULT: THE V10 OPTION
Which is the best solution for F1? V8, V10, or V12? The ideal number of cylinders is a long-standing debate. Based on the same regulations, Ford has elected a V8, Renault, Mercedes, and Peugeot a V10, and Ferrari a V12. Since 1989, when Formula 1 reverted to normally aspirated engines, the V10 blocks of Honda, then Renault, have won six out of seven titles.

In order to do away with pipes, the walls of the cylinder block are cast with internal channels for the circulation of oil and water.

ALUMINUM AND STEEL

WHAT GOES INTO AN ENGINE?

Aluminum is the most commonly used metal in today's F1 engines. Cast iron disappeared completely in the 1980s in favor of aluminum, which is lighter. Aluminum has also replaced magnesium, which corrodes in contact with water. However, steel and titanium have yet to be challenged for those moving parts that must withstand the greatest forces.

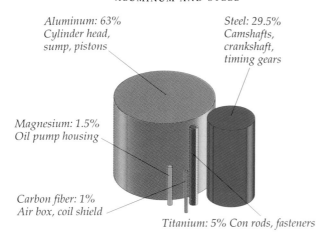

Aluminum: 63%
Cylinder head, sump, pistons

Steel: 29.5%
Camshafts, crankshaft, timing gears

Magnesium: 1.5%
Oil pump housing

Carbon fiber: 1%
Air box, coil shield

Titanium: 5% Con rods, fasteners

Except for certain parts that need to be made from special materials, Formula 1 engines are principally made from aluminum and steel.

EIGHT ENGINES

Eight different engine manufacturers were involved in F1 in 1995: Renault, Ferrari, Ford, Mercedes, Peugeot, Yamaha, Mugen Honda, and Hart. Only Renault enjoyed a partnership association with two teams, Williams and Benetton. All the others worked with a single partner, while some operated on a rental basis with certain teams. This was the case with Hart (Arrows) and Ford (Pacific, Forti, and Minardi).

RENAULT V10
Williams and Benetton

FORD V8
Sauber, Minardi, Pacific, and Forti

MUGEN HONDA V10
Ligier

YAMAHA V10
Tyrrell

HART V8
Arrows

FERRARI V12
Ferrari

MERCEDES V10
McLaren

PEUGEOT V10
Jordan

RENAULT SPORT: A STAFF OF OVER 150 FOR AN ENGINE

A STAFF OF OVER 150 TO BUILD AN ENGINE

Renault Sport employs a total staff of around 150: 28 engineers, 20 draftsmen, 35 engine mechanics, 8 electronics specialists, 20 machinists and fitters, 4 systems engineers, 6 bench technicians, 15 in purchasing, production, and inspection, and 15 administrative staff.

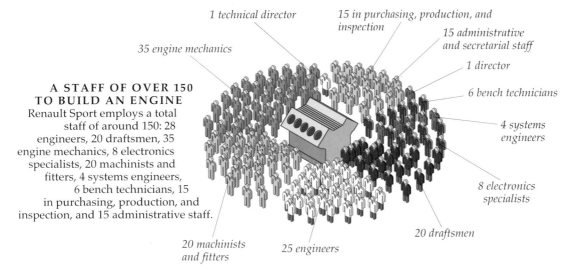

1 technical director

15 in purchasing, production, and inspection

15 administrative and secretarial staff

35 engine mechanics

1 director

6 bench technicians

4 systems engineers

8 electronics specialists

20 machinists and fitters

25 engineers

20 draftsmen

EVOLUTION OF F1 ENGINES

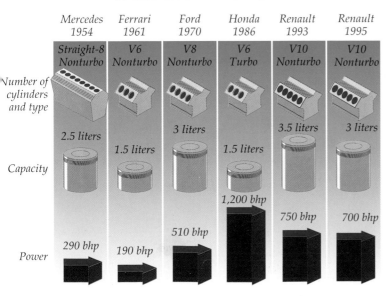

	Mercedes 1954	Ferrari 1961	Ford 1970	Honda 1986	Renault 1993	Renault 1995
Number of cylinders and type	Straight-8 Nonturbo	V6 Nonturbo	V8 Nonturbo	V6 Turbo	V10 Nonturbo	V10 Nonturbo
Capacity	2.5 liters	1.5 liters	3 liters	1.5 liters	3.5 liters	3 liters
Power	290 bhp	190 bhp	510 bhp	1,200 bhp	750 bhp	700 bhp

RENAULT V6 TURBO

This engine changed the face of F1. In 1977, nobody believed that a 1.5-liter turbocharged engine could possibly beat a 3-liter normally aspirated unit. Renault proved it was possible during what became known as the "turbo years" – possibly F1's finest.

TURBO BOOST

Over the years, F1 engines have become more compact, lighter, and more fuel-efficient. At the same time, power outputs have risen, reaching a peak during the turbo years (1977-1988). The leading engines of the day – including BMW, Porsche, Renault, Ferrari, and Honda – put out more than 1,200 bhp in qualifying specification.

Formula 1 engineers

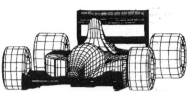

THERE EXIST two distinct types of F1 engineers – those who design engines and those who design the chassis. Engine specialists need the technical backing of a major manufacturer and tend to be loyal – either by nature or necessity – to one firm. Chassis engineers move around more. Whereas before they worked in the shadow of team owners, they have today become aware of their own importance and conscious that their expertise is transferable from one team to another. As a result, they have acquired star status in F1, earning salaries of hundreds of thousands of dollars. A transfer market exists for engineers. At Williams, however, Frank Williams soon recognized Patrick Head's rare talent in 1977 and offered him shares in the team to ensure his loyalty.

TECHNICAL DIRECTOR
This is the highest position an engineer can reach in a team. He is the man who oversees everything. An all-rounder, he establishes the overall program for the specialized engineers – mechanical, aerodynamic, systems, and computation – working under him.

JOHN BARNARD
Ferrari
49, British. Learned his trade with Lola; F1 debut with McLaren in 1981. Returned to Ferrari after a spell at Benetton. Works from his own UK-based premises.

1) SKETCHES
The design of a Formula 1 car starts with sketched ideas on a sheet of paper.

INNOVATIONS THAT HAVE CHANGED F1
From time to time, certain engineers or ideas have provided fresh impetus to F1 design. Here are a few examples which have changed the face of Grand Prix racing.

REAR-MOUNTED ENGINES
Cooper 45, 1958
It was John Cooper who brought a halt to the era of front-mounted engines with the Cooper 45, which took the crown in 1959 and 1960.

WINGS
Brabham BT 26, 1968
Jack Brabham was the first to use movable wings in Formula 1. Outlawed in 1969, they were replaced by fixed wings.

INBOARD SUSPENSION
Lotus 72, 1970
Having designed the first monocoque chassis in 1962, Colin Chapman introduced inboard suspension and side-mounted radiators in 1970.

ROSS BRAWN
Benetton
*41, British. F1 debut with
Williams in 1976 before moving
to FORCE, then Arrows, then
Jaguar in Sports-Prototypes.
Joined Benetton in 1991.*

PATRICK HEAD
Williams
*49, British. The most loyal of them
all. F1 debut with Wolf-Williams
in 1976. Has never left Williams
since and became a partner in
the team in 1977.*

GARY ANDERSON
Jordan
*44, British. Former mechanic with
James Hunt at McLaren. Began
his career by designing an F3 car
before designing the first Jordan
F1 car in 1991.*

NEIL OATLEY
McLaren
*44, British. F1 debut with
Williams in 1977. After a two-
year spell at Lola, moved to
McLaren where he was appointed
Chief Designer in 1989.*

2) COMPUTER
Component parts of the
car are translated into
CAD-CAM language.

TECHNICAL STAFF AT WILLIAMS
*Williams' Technical Director Patrick
Head is very much Frank Williams'
right-hand man. A Chief Designer,
Adrian Newey, and a
number of specialized
engineers work
under his
direction.*

Director: Frank Williams

Technical Director: Patrick Head

Chief
Designer:
Adrian
Newey

Administrative
Director: David
Williams

Manufacturing

Administration

Race and
test teams

Travel coordinator

Facilities

Systems

Logistics

Programming

Personnel

Team Manager:
Richard
Stanford

Design engineers,
research engineers, and
development engineers

Personnel

3) MANUFACTURING
Component parts are manufactured on
computer-programmed machine tools and
finally assembled. A
Formula 1 car
is born!

GROUND EFFECT
Lotus 78, 1977
*Another of Chapman's ideas. The
undertray of the Lotus 78 formed an
upturned wing, forcing the chassis to
the ground. Ground effect had arrived.*

CARBON BODY
McLaren MP4/1, 1982
*When he took over at McLaren in
1982, Ron Dennis pinned his faith
on John Barnard, who produced
Formula 1's first carbon body.*

DATA LOGGING
Renault RE60, 1985
*An onboard electronic pack recorded
revs, pressures, and temperatures. More
recently, telemetry allowed this data to
be transmitted in real time to the pits.*

RAISED NOSES
March 881, 1988
*Raised noses, first seen in
1988, were the idea of Adrian
Newey to improve air flow
past the chassis.*

Fuel and tires

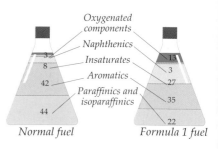

Oxygenated
components
Naphthenics
Insaturates
Aromatics
Paraffinics and
isoparaffinics

32
8
42

44

15
3
27
35

22

Normal fuel   *Formula 1 fuel*

FORMULA 1 CARS USE neither the same tires nor the same fuels as road cars. Racing rubber has nothing in common with ordinary tires but the gasoline used in F1 does bear a resemblance to blends sold at the pump. While the basic ingredients are the same, the exact formula of competition fuel differs in order to adapt it to the demands of racing engines. Performance, however, does not come cheap. A liter of fuel costs at least two dollars and a racing tire will set you back around $1,000.

**ALCHEMY
AND PERFORMANCE**
The same ingredients go into the fuels that power Formula 1 cars and those available at your local service station. Only the proportions differ.

SPECIAL COMPOUNDS

Tire technology has made enormous progress since the early part of the century, when motorists ran on rubberized canvas strips. These extremely rigid tires had a habit of breaking up. Today, the exact formulas used in tire manufacture are closely guarded secrets, but principal ingredients include rubber, carbon black, oils, sulfur, and additives.

1915

1960

PERFORMANCE TEMPERATURE

Formula 1 tires offer optimum grip at temperatures of about 212°F (100°C). This is why special warmers are used to preheat the tires just before they are fitted to the cars. Even so, a full lap must be completed before a tire reaches peak performance. A technician checks the temperature of the tires at each pit stop.

FROM ROAD TIRES TO SPECIALIZED RACING RUBBER

The development of special tires for racing purposes is a fairly recent phenomenon. The first trials took place at the American circuit of Daytona in 1957 and their use became general practice in 1962.

ELF IN POLE POSITION

Elf – the fuel of World Champions. In 1995, Elf dominated its rivals for the fifth consecutive season. Research chemists at Elf's Solaize laboratories near Lyons blend special fuels not only for each type of engine, but for each of their respective evolutions. This advanced research work has directly benefited ordinary commercial fuels. In fact, in line with F1 regulations, Grand Prix fuels are very close to those retailed in service stations.

FIERCE COMPETITION

For fuel companies, F1 is an effective means of promoting their image. In 1995, five companies – Elf, Agip, Sasol, BP, and Total – supplied the F1 grid, and rivalry between them is as fierce as that between teams. Since 1994, however, another battle has been raging: that of lubricants. Having been checked by the FIA in their development of exclusive fuels, oil companies have focused on high-performance engine and transmission oils. This is a new aid for engine manufacturers whose constant endeavor is to take engine speeds increasingly higher.

Dry-weather slick, 1995

Wet-weather tire, 1995

WET AND DRY

The ingredients that go into the manufacture of a Formula 1 tire have only one purpose – to provide maximum grip in all surface conditions. In 1995, Goodyear's slick tires came in four compounds ranging from "A" (hard) to "D" (very soft). For wet weather, a fifth option is available featuring a very soft compound and a tread pattern capable of clearing 26 liters of water per second at speeds of up to 300 km/h. F1 tires are tubeless and pressures used vary from 1 to 1.4 bars.

FLAT SPOT

Locked wheels under braking can cause irreparable damage to tires. The soft compound rubber instantly overheats and sticks to the track, causing what is known as a flat spot on the tire's surface.

Formula 1 comparisons

Price in France in 1995: FRF 59,500
Length: 343 cm, width: 163 cm

Price in France in 1995: FRF 200,000
Length: 380 cm, width: 183 cm

Price in 1995: approx. FRF 4,000,000
Length: 420 cm, width: 200 cm

Wʜᴀᴛ ᴅᴏ ᴀ ʀᴇɴᴀᴜʟᴛ ᴛᴡɪɴɢᴏ, a Renault Spider, and a Williams F1 racing car have in common? Answer: four wheels, a steering wheel, and a Renault engine. And that's about all. A Formula 1 car is designed to go as fast as possible over a very short distance. The distance of a Grand Prix is 300 km. Should a Formula 1 car break during the 301st kilometer, having passed the checkered flag, then it has done its job. On the other hand, a Twingo or a Renault Spider must be capable of exceeding 100,000 kilometers without difficulty.

TWINGO With David Coulthard at the wheel, the Twingo took Club Corner at Silverstone at a speed of 80 km/h.

SPIDER Same day, same circuit, same corner, same driver. 110 km/h for the Renault Spider.

80 km/h

SPEED
Wide tires and wings – which have a braking effect through air – make F1 cars more agile than quick, although the top speed of the Spider is 130 km/h lower than the Williams-Renault. At Le Mans, Sports-Prototype cars have been known to exceed 400 km/h along the celebrated Hunaudières straight.

TOP SPEED

Twingo: 150 km/h

Spider: 210 km/h

Williams-Renault: 340 km/h

ACCELERATION
If a Twingo, a Spider, and a Formula 1 car set off for a standing-start kilometer at the same moment, the F1 car would cover the distance in 12 seconds. In that time, the Spider would have covered 215 meters and the Twingo just 105 meters. The Spider would pass the line in 27.5s, the Twingo in 36s.

FROM STATIONARY

Start	250m	500m	750m	1,000m

Twingo: 105m in 12s

Spider: 215m in 12s

Williams-Renault: 1,000m in 12s

BRAKING
Thanks to its light weight, carbon discs, and broad tires, a Formula 1 car is unbeatable when it comes to braking, requiring just 18 meters to brake from 100 km/h to a standstill.

BRAKING FROM 100 TO 0 KPH

Spider: 37m

Twingo: 46m

Williams-Renault: 18m

Meters

50
40
30
20
10

WILLIAMS-RENAULT

F1 rear tire
Width: 38 cm
Height: 66 cm

Front tire
Width: 29 cm
Height: 64 cm

F1 engine:
8, 10, or
12 cylinders,
3,000 cc,
approx. 700 bhp

MAXIMUM POWER
Formula 1 engine manufacturers do not like to reveal exact power values for their creations. In the case of the most powerful engines, maximum power is near the 700 bhp mark. While outright power does of course influence a Formula 1 car's top speed, other criteria for evaluating an engine's performance exist, such as its flexibility or the availability of power across the entire rev-band. A peaky engine, or one that is too bulky or heavy, can upset the balance of a chassis. Nonetheless, maximum power is probably the most readily understood benchmark. With a cubic capacity two-and-a-half times that of the Twingo, an F1 engine is 14 times more powerful.

SPIDER

Rear tire
Width: 22.5 cm
Height: 61.5 cm

Front tire
Width: 20.5 cm
Height: 61.5 cm

Engine:
4 cylinders,
1,998 cc,
150 bhp

TWINGO

Rear tire
Width: 14.5 cm
Height: 54 cm

Front tire
Width: 14.5 cm
Height: 54 cm

Engine:
4 cylinders,
1,239 cc,
55 bhp

WILLIAMS-RENAULT FW17 The following day, but in identical weather conditions, David Coulthard's Williams-Renault took the Club Corner at a speed of 160 km/h during official practice for the British Grand Prix.

110 km/h

160 km/h

FUEL CONSUMPTION
A Formula 1 engine is a real guzzler. At top-speed, 80 liters of fuel are needed to cover 100 km, eight times the requirement of a Twingo. During a Grand Prix, a Formula 1 car consumes around 180 liters in a distance of 300 km.

FUEL CONSUMPTION FOR 100 KILOMETERS AT TOP SPEED

Williams-Renault: 80 liters

Spider: 26 liters

Twingo: 10.4 liters

POWER-TO-WEIGHT RATIO
A Formula 1 car boasts 1 bhp for every 750 grams of weight. For the Spider, 1 bhp has to pull 5 kg while the same figure for the Twingo is 14 kg. The power-to-weight ratio goes a long way toward explaining the staggering performance of a Formula 1 car. A Williams-Renault tips the scales at just 520 kg, including 5 kg mandatory ballast if not carrying an onboard TV camera.

Twingo: 14.4 kg/bhp (790 kg, 55 bhp)

Spider: 5.25 kg/bhp (790 kg, 150 bhp)

Williams-Renault: 0.743 kg/bhp (520 kg, 700 bhp)

F1 on the move

As it works its way around the circuits of the world, Formula 1 is like a small town on the move. Each team travels with two, sometimes three transporters, plus one, two, or even three motorhomes that bear the names of sponsors and serve as base for team personnel and guests. Nothing is spared in the decoration of these gleaming vehicles, and their cost runs into hundreds of thousands of dollars. A Grand Prix paddock is a spectacle in its own right! For Grands Prix outside Europe, equipment is freighted in by specially chartered planes to be stored in crates at the circuits.

THE TRANSPORTATION BUDGET

To assist teams with the considerable costs involved in transporting personnel and equipment to races (a budget of around $3,000,000 for a middle-of-the-grid team), the Formula 1 Constructors' Association (FOCA) takes on board a share of the expenses incurred by the ten best-placed teams in the championship.

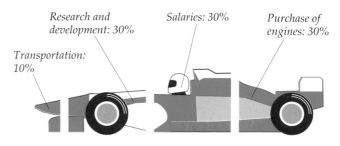

Research and development: 30%

Salaries: 30%

Purchase of engines: 30%

Transportation: 10%

THE RACING TEAM'S BUDGET

UNLOADING

During transportation, cars are stowed on upper decks. They are unloaded using an electric tail-lift that also serves as a door when folded in the upright position.

FORMULA 1 HAS PUT ON WEIGHT

Since 1950, the amount of equipment shipped to races for two cars has increased ten-fold. This increase is due to the number of spares carried.

Ferrari
2.5 tons of equipment

McLaren-Ford
6 tons of equipment

Benetton-Renault
25 tons of equipment

1950

1970

1995

CUSTOMS CLEARANCE

Formula 1 hates wasting time. Equipment shipped from one circuit to another must be able to pass from country to country with the least fuss possible. It is the team's logistics manager who is responsible for carrying with him the piles of administrative documents required by customs officials, and he never lets them out of his sight.

ENGINES APART

Only one team, Ferrari, produces both its own chassis and engines. All other teams are made up of a chassis manufacturer and an associate engine supplier. In the case of Williams and Benetton, racing cars arrive at the circuit with engines already fitted, while spare blocks are shipped independently from Renault Sport's Viry-Châtillon base near Paris. The two meet up at the circuit where mechanics from the two teams pick up the seven precious V10s that they will use over the weekend from the Renault truck. Crates for the attention of Williams are marked with a gray "W," those for Benetton with a blue "B."

PELL-MELL

Twenty years ago, tools, spares, cars, and occasionally cots for mechanics, were loaded onto trucks pell-mell. Today's semitrailers are made-to-order affairs with air-conditioning to ensure pleasant working conditions at all times.

Trucks and trailers are painted in the colors of the team

TAKING STOCK

In addition to cars and engines, leading teams such as Benetton-Renault ship practically their entire workshop to the venue of each Grand Prix. Semitrailers are filled to the brim with sufficient parts to build a complete car many times over. Equipment includes:

- body-parts: front and rear wings, undertrays, nose cones, repair kits (resin)
- telemetry: aerials, computers, calculators, color screens, printers
- electrical equipment: generators, voltage regulators
- compressors and oxygen bottles for air tools
- a few hundred kilograms of miscellaneous tools
- and even spares to repair...imagine the crates that contain all this!

OPERATING THEATER

Team transporters are as spotless and tidy as operating theaters. The tools and hardware – screws and fasteners, for example – necessary for the assembly and maintenance of the cars are stored beneath benches along the sides of the trailer. Once the cars themselves have been unloaded, mechanics and engineers have a fully fitted workshop at their disposal.

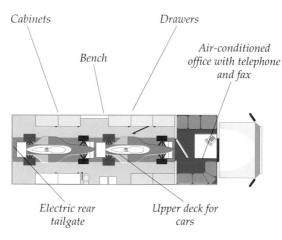

Cabinets

Drawers

Bench

Air-conditioned office with telephone and fax

Electric rear tailgate

Upper deck for cars

FOUR TIMES AROUND THE WORLD

A Formula 1 team clocks up some 160,000 kilometers every year, the equivalent of four times around the planet. The 50 or so people who make up the race team spend an average of 200 hours each season traveling in planes.

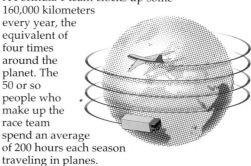

Formula 1 circuits

In 45 years, F1 has visited 57 circuits in 23 countries. Since 1984, the number of Grands Prix organized in a single season has been limited to 16, although the FIA accepted 17 rounds in 1995. Theoretically, individual countries are able to host just one race, although there are exceptions to this rule. The patronage of San Marino, for example, allows Imola to run a second race in Italy, while a second Grand Prix is organized in Japan under the label "Pacific Grand Prix." The introduction by the FIA of strict safety standards coincided with the disappearance of such legendary circuits as Brands Hatch and Zandvoort.

NUMBER OF GRANDS PRIX HOSTED PER CIRCUIT SINCE 1950

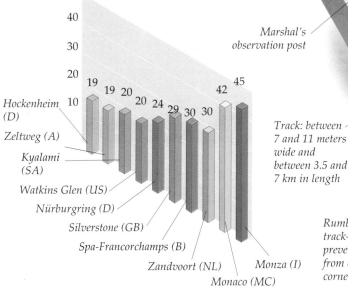

- 19 Hockenheim (D)
- 19 Zeltweg (A)
- 20 Kyalami (SA)
- 20 Watkins Glen (US)
- 24 Nürburgring (D)
- 29 Silverstone (GB)
- 30 Spa-Francorchamps (B)
- 30 Zandvoort (NL)
- 42 Monaco (MC)
- 45 Monza (I)

Monaco, Spa, Silverstone, and Monza all hosted races in the first ever F1 World Championship in 1950. Although their layouts have since been revised, these four circuits have held the highest number of races in the sport's history.

CIRCUIT FACILITIES
A Formula 1 circuit is visited annually by inspectors to ensure that mandatory FIA requirements are met.

Giant television screens: located by the main grandstands, these allow spectators to follow the entire race.

Camera

Stand

Marshal's observation post

Track: between 7 and 11 meters wide and between 3.5 and 7 km in length

Rumble strips: track-side curbs prevent drivers from cutting corners.

Camera

First corner: to avoid tangles, the first corner must be a constant- or widening-radius curve. Cars must be able to take it at 125 km/h.

1995 CALENDAR

Brazil
Interlagos
March 26, 1995
4.325 km

Argentina
Buenos Aires
April 9, 1995
4.259 km

San Marino
Imola
April 30, 1995
5.040 km

Spain
Barcelona
May 14, 1995
4.747 km

Monaco
Monte-Carlo
May 28, 1995
3.328 km

Canada
Montréal
June 11, 1995
4.430 km

France
Magny-Cours
July 2, 1995
4.271 km

Great Britain
Silverstone
July 16, 1995
5.226 km

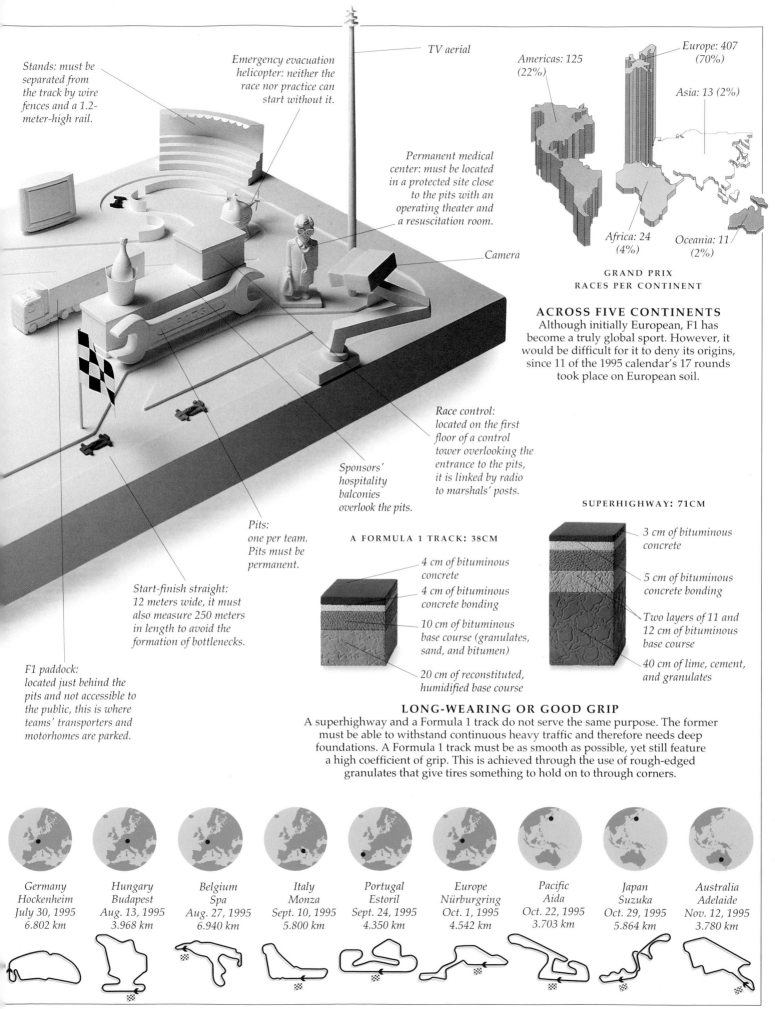

Stands: must be separated from the track by wire fences and a 1.2-meter-high rail.

Emergency evacuation helicopter: neither the race nor practice can start without it.

TV aerial

Permanent medical center: must be located in a protected site close to the pits with an operating theater and a resuscitation room.

Camera

Americas: 125 (22%)

Europe: 407 (70%)

Asia: 13 (2%)

Africa: 24 (4%)

Oceania: 11 (2%)

GRAND PRIX RACES PER CONTINENT

ACROSS FIVE CONTINENTS
Although initially European, F1 has become a truly global sport. However, it would be difficult for it to deny its origins, since 11 of the 1995 calendar's 17 rounds took place on European soil.

Race control: located on the first floor of a control tower overlooking the entrance to the pits, it is linked by radio to marshals' posts.

Sponsors' hospitality balconies overlook the pits.

Pits: one per team. Pits must be permanent.

Start-finish straight: 12 meters wide, it must also measure 250 meters in length to avoid the formation of bottlenecks.

F1 paddock: located just behind the pits and not accessible to the public, this is where teams' transporters and motorhomes are parked.

SUPERHIGHWAY: 71CM

3 cm of bituminous concrete

5 cm of bituminous concrete bonding

Two layers of 11 and 12 cm of bituminous base course

40 cm of lime, cement, and granulates

A FORMULA 1 TRACK: 38CM

4 cm of bituminous concrete

4 cm of bituminous concrete bonding

10 cm of bituminous base course (granulates, sand, and bitumen)

20 cm of reconstituted, humidified base course

LONG-WEARING OR GOOD GRIP
A superhighway and a Formula 1 track do not serve the same purpose. The former must be able to withstand continuous heavy traffic and therefore needs deep foundations. A Formula 1 track must be as smooth as possible, yet still feature a high coefficient of grip. This is achieved through the use of rough-edged granulates that give tires something to hold on to through corners.

Germany
Hockenheim
July 30, 1995
6.802 km

Hungary
Budapest
Aug. 13, 1995
3.968 km

Belgium
Spa
Aug. 27, 1995
6.940 km

Italy
Monza
Sept. 10, 1995
5.800 km

Portugal
Estoril
Sept. 24, 1995
4.350 km

Europe
Nürburgring
Oct. 1, 1995
4.542 km

Pacific
Aida
Oct. 22, 1995
3.703 km

Japan
Suzuka
Oct. 29, 1995
5.864 km

Australia
Adelaide
Nov. 12, 1995
3.780 km

Officials

Max Mosley
FIA President

A FORMULA 1 GRAND PRIX could not be organized without the presence of FIA officials. As representatives of motorsport's international governing body, these are the people who ensure that regulations are complied with at all times. Their individual roles are specified in the "Yellow Book," an indispensable bible composed of nearly 850 pages of regulations covering all aspects of motorsport events organized under the jurisdiction of the Fédération Internationale de l'Automobile. Certain officials work full-time for the FIA and attend all F1 meetings. Others are nominated for individual races by the national governing body of the country hosting the race. The following provides a brief insight into the functions of the principal ones.

EVENT DIRECTOR
The Event Director is responsible for the smooth overall running of the meeting. Constantly in contact with all other officials, his duties include checking competition numbers, ensuring that cars are correctly positioned on the grid, chairing a Drivers' Briefing on the morning before the race, and recommending penalties for anyone failing to comply with regulations. He is the most important individual at a meeting.

MEDICAL OFFICER
A Chief Medical Officer, Dr. Sid Watkins, has been nominated by the FIA to attend all World Championship races, where his role is to supervise all medical matters.

THE STARTER
Belgium's Roland Bruynseraede has been responsible for "unleashing the pack" at all Grand Prix races since 1987. Roland is also Race Director and Chairman of the FIA's Safety Delegate.

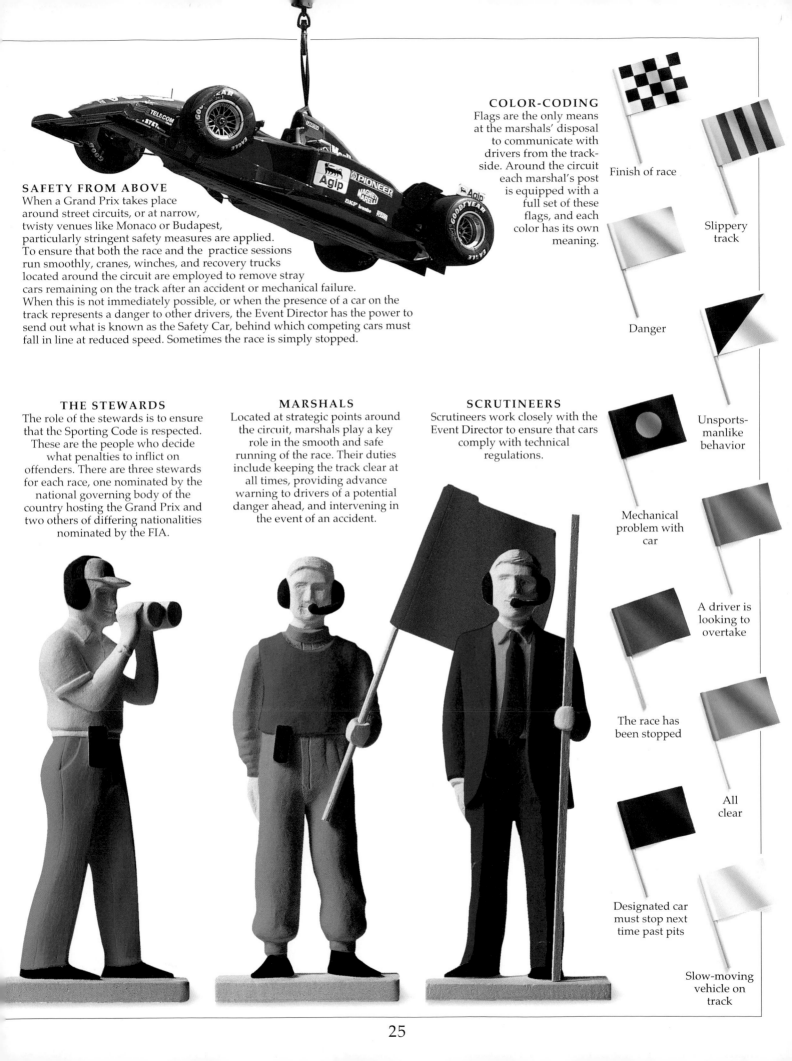

SAFETY FROM ABOVE

When a Grand Prix takes place around street circuits, or at narrow, twisty venues like Monaco or Budapest, particularly stringent safety measures are applied. To ensure that both the race and the practice sessions run smoothly, cranes, winches, and recovery trucks located around the circuit are employed to remove stray cars remaining on the track after an accident or mechanical failure. When this is not immediately possible, or when the presence of a car on the track represents a danger to other drivers, the Event Director has the power to send out what is known as the Safety Car, behind which competing cars must fall in line at reduced speed. Sometimes the race is simply stopped.

COLOR-CODING

Flags are the only means at the marshals' disposal to communicate with drivers from the track-side. Around the circuit each marshal's post is equipped with a full set of these flags, and each color has its own meaning.

Finish of race

Slippery track

Danger

THE STEWARDS

The role of the stewards is to ensure that the Sporting Code is respected. These are the people who decide what penalties to inflict on offenders. There are three stewards for each race, one nominated by the national governing body of the country hosting the Grand Prix and two others of differing nationalities nominated by the FIA.

MARSHALS

Located at strategic points around the circuit, marshals play a key role in the smooth and safe running of the race. Their duties include keeping the track clear at all times, providing advance warning to drivers of a potential danger ahead, and intervening in the event of an accident.

SCRUTINEERS

Scrutineers work closely with the Event Director to ensure that cars comply with technical regulations.

Unsports-
manlike
behavior

Mechanical
problem with
car

A driver is
looking to
overtake

The race has
been stopped

All
clear

Designated car
must stop next
time past pits

Slow-moving
vehicle on
track

Life in the pits

TEAMS WILL BEGIN TO ARRIVE at a circuit on the Wednesday preceding the race and leave again on the Sunday evening. Each team works out of pits allocated to teams on the basis of their position in the previous year's World Championship, and this order does not change once the season is under way. For four days the pits are a buzz of activity. Entry is strictly controlled and even the media and photographers do not escape surveillance. Telemetry monitors are hidden away at the back of the pits behind tarpaulin enclosures. Mechanics continue to work on cars during the evening and into the night, well after the last spectator has left the circuit.

0600	Wake up
0700	Set off for the racetrack
0730	Arrive at the racetrack
0735	Preparing the car
0920	Fitting wheels and nose cone
0930	Free practice, adjustments
1100	End of session, checking
1120	Snack
1130	Preparing car for timed laps
1300	Official timed practice
1400	Draining gasoline and oil
1500	Lunch
1530	Preparing the car for the race: changing engine, suspension, transmission, wheel bearings, radiators
2230	Dinner
2400	Return to the hotel

A DAY IN THE LIFE
In the course of a Grand Prix, team mechanics will spend a minimum of 16 hours per day at the circuit. Both lunch and dinner are taken at the circuit. Should a car be damaged during practice, mechanics might even have to work through the night to carry out necessary repairs. They fly home on the Sunday evening in order to be back at work the following morning.

A HIVE OF ACTIVITY
At a Grand Prix, the pits tend to resemble a busy beehive. Some 50 people, from the drivers themselves to the security guard, work in the Williams pits at any one time.

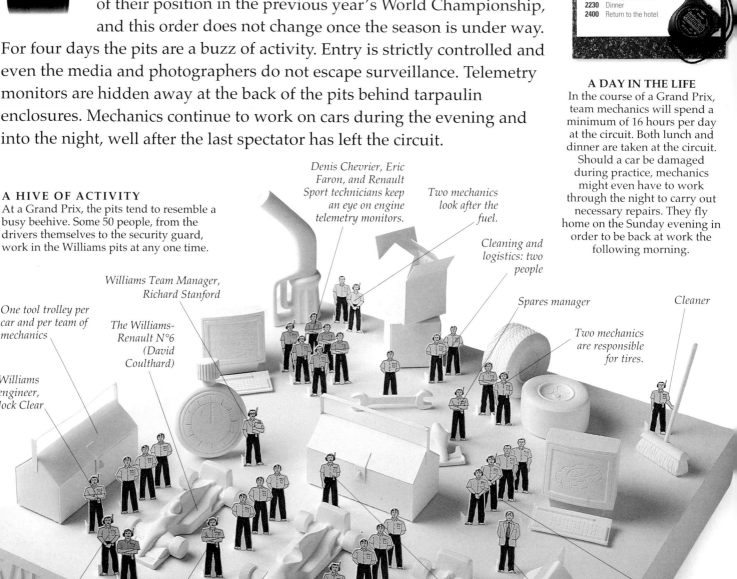

Denis Chevrier, Eric Faron, and Renault Sport technicians keep an eye on engine telemetry monitors.

Two mechanics look after the fuel.

Cleaning and logistics: two people

Spares manager

Cleaner

Two mechanics are responsible for tires.

Williams Team Manager, Richard Stanford

One tool trolley per car and per team of mechanics

The Williams-Renault N°6 (David Coulthard)

Williams engineer, Jock Clear

Four Williams technicians keep a watch on transmission and suspension telemetry monitors.

Security guard

Frank Williams

The Williams-Renault N°5 (Damon Hill)

Williams Chief Designer, Adrian Newey

Renault Sport MD, Christian Contzen

Four mechanics are assigned to each car.

Spare car

Williams Engineer David Brown

Renault Sport Technical Director, Bernard Dudot

Williams Technical Director, Patrick Head

Radios permit team managers to communicate with drivers and to issue instructions to mechanics once the race is underway.

Woolen gloves protect hands against heat during tire changes.

The return of mid-race refueling in 1994 has led to mechanics wearing flame-resistant overalls and helmets during pit stops

TEAM CLOTHING

Light shirts and shorts in hot weather, long pants for cooler climates. The traditional oily overalls that F1 mechanics used to wear were dropped a long time ago in favor of today's more dashing team clothing, more in keeping with the high-tech image of F1. However, the return of mid-race refueling in 1994 has led to mechanics wearing flame-resistant overalls and helmets during pit stops, just like their Indy racing counterparts.

In Formula 1, team colors have even found their way onto footwear

SWIFT 'N' SURE
Formula 1 mechanics are the fastest in the world. The outcome of a race can often depend on the swiftness and reliability of their work.

ENGINE
An emergency engine swap takes one hour.

TRANSMISSION
A transmission takes just half an hour to change.

SHOCK ABSORBERS
Twelve minutes to change all four shock absorbers...

PEDAL BOX
... and just ten minutes to fit pedal box, seat, and harness into the spare car.

ARROWS	BENETTON	FERRARI	FORTI	JORDAN	LIGIER

McLAREN	MINARDI	PACIFIC	SAUBER	TYRRELL	WILLIAMS

PIT CREW CLOTHING
Clothing worn by mechanics and engineers uses the colors of the team's main sponsors. Teams even supply personnel with official travel-wear – significantly more discreet – for travel by plane from one race to another.

Televised coverage of the race

Lap-by-lap positions and times

Engine telemetry data

UMBRELLAS UP
As cars wait on the grid before the start, a team member holds an umbrella over the driver's head. Besides protecting from rain or sun, it also provides an extra opportunity to get sponsors' names in a photograph.

TV MONITORS
To keep a permanent eye on the performance of his car, an engine technician has three screens at his disposal. The first displays a variety of technical data concerning the engine's performance, a television monitor allows him to follow the race itself, and a third screen provides lap times and positions.

Formula 1 drivers

Rᴇᴀᴄʜɪɴɢ ᴛʜᴇ ᴛᴏᴘ ᴏғ ᴛʜᴇ ꜰ1 ʟᴀᴅᴅᴇʀ takes talent, courage… and a degree of luck. The statistics suggest that your chances of success are better if you start young and are a national of a country where motorsports have a deeply rooted tradition. Of the 564 drivers from 31 different countries to have started a Grand Prix since the creation of the World Championship in 1950, half of them – and 13 of the 26 drivers who started the 1995 season – hailed from the UK, Italy, or France. This is no coincidence: racing is a way of life in these three countries and young talent gets a real opportunity to come to the fore. Like tennis and football, F1 has not escaped the baby-champion phenomenon. At the age of just 14, more than half of today's grid were already out racing karts. Gone are the days when the likes of Graham Hill could pass their driving test at the age of 24 and go on to become World Champion…twice!

NATIONALITIES OF F1 DRIVERS (1950-1995)

France : 65 (12%)
Great Britain: 137 (24%)
Switzerland: 21 (4%)
Germany: 38 (7%)
Belgium: 20 (4%)
Italy: 77 (14%)
US: 44 (8%)
Rest of world: 107 (17%)
Brazil : 18 (3%)
Argentina: 19 (4%)
South Africa: 18 (3%)

THE 1995 LINE-UP

Twenty-six drivers lined up for the start of the opening round of the 1995 season. However, the situation evolved considerably in the course of the year. Wendlinger lost his drive at Sauber after just four races – to give France's Jean-Christophe Boullion a foot in the door – while Suzuki and Brundle shared the same Ligier. Meanwhile, the mid-season withdrawal of the Simtek team provisionally deprived Verstappen and Schiatarella of drives. Job security in F1 does not exist.

WHERE DO THEY COME FROM?

Since the creation of Formula 1, one driver in four has been British, one in two has hailed from Great Britain, France, or Italy, while three out of four were European-born. At the other end of the scale, five countries have produced just one Formula 1 driver: Thailand, Morocco, Liechtenstein, Chile, Columbia, and Monaco.

JEAN ALESI
31, France
Ferrari

LUCA BADOER
25, Italy
Minardi

RUBENS BARRICHELLO
23, Brazil
Jordan

GERHARD BERGER
36, Austria
Ferrari

MARK BLUNDELL
29, GB
McLaren

JEAN-CHRISTOPHE BOULLION
26, France
Sauber

MARTIN BRUNDLE
36, GB
Ligier

TAKI INOUE
32, Japan
Arrows

EDDIE IRVINE
30, GB
Jordan

UKYO KATAYAMA
30, Japan
Tyrrell

PIERLUIGI MARTINI
34, Italy
Minardi

ANDREA MONTERMINI
31, Italy
Pacific

GIANNI MORBIDELLI
28, Italy
Arrows

ROBERTO MORENO
37, Brazil
Forti

KART KIDS

Eighteen of the 26 drivers who started the 1995 season, including Schumacher, Alesi, and Hakkinen, began their careers racing karts.
Initially considered racing's poorer cousin and a sport that encouraged bad reflexes, karting eventually came of age in the 1970s when it produced champions of the caliber of Fittipaldi and Peterson. They were eloquent proof that a successful background in karts could genuinely help launch a career in F1.

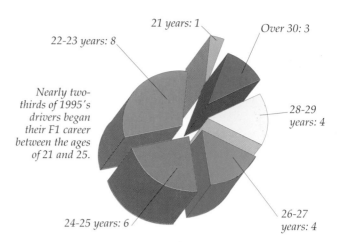

Nearly two-thirds of 1995's drivers began their F1 career between the ages of 21 and 25.

21 years: 1
22-23 years: 8
Over 30: 3
28-29 years: 4
26-27 years: 4
24-25 years: 6

**AGES OF 1995'S DRIVERS
AT THE TIME OF THEIR FORMULA 1 DEBUT**

DRIVING SCHOLARSHIPS

Competition driving schools exist in many countries, but the French system has proved a particularly successful model in which the prize is often a season of single-seater racing. Of the 22 French drivers to have reached F1 in the past decade, 13 were former scholarship winners, including Prost, Tambay, Arnoux, and Panis. Not winning the scholarship does not necessarily spell the end of a racing career. Alliot and Laffite were beaten in their respective finals, while Alesi and Gachot were both dominated by Eric Bernard during one hotly disputed year.

SINGLE-MAKE FORMULAS

Formula Renault, Formula Ford, and Formula Opel-Vauxhall exist in many European countries, while Formula Fiat enjoys popular success in Italy. The leading manufacturers involved in motorsport have long organized such promotional formulas aimed at giving young drivers a chance to cut their teeth at low cost. Prost won the French Formula Renault Championship when he was just 21, and Senna left his mark on the British Formula Ford Championship.

**DAVID
COULTHARD**
*25, GB
Williams*

**PEDRO
DINIZ**
*25, Brazil
Forti*

**HEINZ-HARALD
FRENTZEN**
*28, Germany
Sauber*

**BERTRAND
GACHOT**
*33, France
Pacific*

**MIKA
HAKKINEN**
*27, Finland
McLaren*

**JOHNNY
HERBERT**
*32, GB
Benetton*

**DAMON
HILL**
*35, GB
Williams*

**OLIVIER
PANIS**
*29, France
Ligier*

**MIKA
SALO**
*29, Finland
Tyrrell*

**DOMENICO
SCHIATTARELLA**
*28, Italy
Simtek*

**MICHAEL
SCHUMACHER**
*27, Germany
Benetton*

**AGURI
SUZUKI**
*35, Japan
Ligier*

**JOS
VERSTAPPEN**
*24, Holland
Simtek*

**KARL
WENDLINGER**
*27, Austria
Sauber*

Driver racewear

Bᴀᴄᴋ ɪɴ 1950, the likes of Fangio and Ascari used to race in shirtsleeves and long pants. Mike Hawthorn even went so far as to sport a bow tie! When an accident occurred – and alas they were all too frequent – the fate of a driver was often in the lap of the gods. All that is history now. Today's textiles have made staggering progress and modern drivers must wear special clothing bearing the international motorsport governing body's tag of approval. Indeed, the FIA's standards are extremely high in this domain, especially concerning flame resistance. A fully-clothed driver must be able to escape unscathed if caught for up to 12 seconds in a 1,300°F (700°C) hydrocarbon blaze.

THE HELMET
Each driver gets through as many as 15 helmets in the course of a season. Besides providing effective head protection, they also sport the driver's personal colors and those of his sponsors.

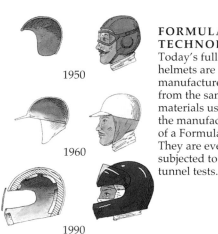

1950

1960

1990

FORMULA 1 TECHNOLOGY
Today's full-face helmets are manufactured from the same materials used in the manufacture of a Formula 1 car. They are even subjected to wind-tunnel tests.

EARPLUGS
Special earplugs housing radio earpieces protect drivers' eardrums from the pounding noise of the engine, which can be as loud as a fighter jet on takeoff.

NECK STRAP AND COLLAR
This limits head movement and prevents neck muscle fatigue at circuits with long, fast corners.

BALACLAVA
The fire-resistant cloth provides added protection against fire.

FROM LEATHER TO NOMEX
In 1950, drivers wore simple leather headgear that afforded excellent protection only against the wind. This was later replaced by helmets made first from papier-mâché, then fiberglass. A modern full-face helmet weighs just 1.2 kg, half the weight of the first models that appeared back in 1968. The Lexan visor, which has replaced the glass goggles of yesteryear, will protect against a stone catapulted at 500 km/h.

EVOLUTION
Since the creation of the World Championship, driver overalls have evolved as much as the cars. The textiles used are the fruit of space research and have increasingly replaced cotton, which protected against little more than the wind!

PROTECTION
Thanks to impact-absorbing helmets and flame-resistant overalls, drivers are no longer without protection in the event of an accident.

Jean Alesi   *Luca Badoer*   *Rubens Barrichello*   *Gerhard Berger*   *Mark Blundell*   *Martin Brundle*   *J-C Boullion*   *David Coulthard*   *Pedro Diniz*   *H-H Frentzen*   *Bertrand Gachot*   *Mika Hakkinen*   *Johnny Herbert*   *Damon Hill*

HOT UNDIES
Driver underwear isn't in the least suggestive and, even in the case of women drivers, lace frills are out of the question. Because of its flame-resistant qualities, Nomex is the only authorized material. Socks, T-shirt, and long underwear are mandatory underneath overalls.

A STEADY HAND
Nomex gloves provide the best protection against fire. Palms are trimmed in leather to ensure optimum grip on the suede steering wheel. Gloves are worn very tight and held in place with a Velcro strap.

NOMEX ARMOR
A driver's overalls are his main line of defense against burns. Tailored from flame-resistant Nomex cloth, they guarantee protection for 12 seconds in a hydrocarbon blaze at 1,300°F (700°C). All threads, and even advertising patches, must meet the same standards.

FOOT SURE
Race shoes are made from leather and are padded with foam to protect against knocks in the cockpit. For maximum fire resistance, they are finished in Nomex and soles are made from high-grip rubber.

| Taki Inoue | Eddie Irvine | Ukyo Katayama | Pierluigi Martini | Andrea Montermini | Gianni Morbidelli | Roberto Moreno | Olivier Panis | Mika Salo | Domenico Schiattarella | Michaël Schumacher | Aguri Suzuki | Jos Verstappen | Karl Wendlinger |

31

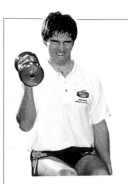

Athletes in their own right

Mᴀᴋᴇ ɴᴏ ᴍɪsᴛᴀᴋᴇ, keeping a Formula 1 car on the track at speeds of up to 300 km/h is a physically exhausting business requiring considerable strength and stamina. The likes of Hill, Schumacher, and Collard, shown here, are all genuine athletes in their own right and devote between three and five hours daily to physical training. Muscle-building – especially of the arms, neck, back, and stomach – helps cope with centrifugal force which, literally, can take your breath away and can put the neck under tremendous strain through fast corners. Special attention is also paid to physical resistance and endurance. Over a Grand Prix distance, drivers supply an effort which can be as intense and exhausting as that required from a semimarathon runner. Last, but not least, comes mental preparation: controlling feelings and maintaining concentration have become critical factors in peak performance. Half the battle of winning pole position is in the mind.…

MADE-TO-MEASURE MUSCLES
An effort of 20 kg is required to turn the steering wheel of a Formula 1 car traveling at a speed of 300 km/h. This simulator – developed by the Paris-based IBSV (Institut Biomédical Sport et Vie) – enables drivers to keep in shape between races.

SUSTAINING THE EFFORT
To evaluate a driver's physical fitness, one of the more commonly used tests involves measuring the maximum amount of oxygen used while cycling on an exercise bike. A fit athlete uses oxygen more efficiently than a sedentary person, a faculty which makes him able to respond more easily when sustained effort is required.

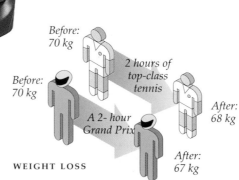

Before: 70 kg

2 hours of top-class tennis

Before: 70 kg

After: 68 kg

A 2-hour Grand Prix

After: 67 kg

WEIGHT LOSS

AN EXHAUSTING BUSINESS
Even for the fittest of drivers, a Formula 1 Grand Prix is an exhausting exercise. On top of fatigue resulting from intense physical effort, drivers also suffer from the effects of acceleration, vibration, and heat. Cockpits are generally 18°F (10°C) hotter than the outside temperature.

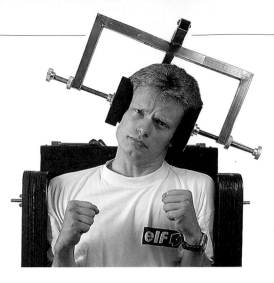

TAKING THE STRAIN

The above machine measures the strength of neck muscles. The driver pushes with his neck alternately to the left and right as hard as he can while the machine records the rate at which fatigue sets in. Neck muscles are subjected to considerable strain under cornering. Centrifugal forces can multiply the weight of the head and helmet by a factor of up to four!

170
160
150
140

Beats per minute

Starting line   *Finish line*

HEARTBEAT

The above cardiac printout is that of Philippe Alliot during a lap of Estoril in Portugal. The peaks correspond to zones of braking into corners and the troughs show where the French driver was able to recover along the straights. In a test involving similar levels of effort back at the clinic, Alliot's average heartbeat would probably not exceed 130 beats per minute compared with the 160 recorded on the graph. The difference is due to the stress of driving a Formula 1 car.

STEERING CLEAR OF EXCESS

To ensure the most balanced diet possible, Formula 1 drivers banish all forms of excess. Alcohol and stimulants – coffee, cola-based drinks – are out of the question, and fat intake is kept to an absolute minimum. Main courses generally consist of grilled white meat or fish served with vegetables, rice, or pasta. Indeed, drivers tend to be big consumers of pasta products since they are a valuable source of slow-burning sugars, which means energy is released progressively for greater endurance. As for doping, no case has ever been recorded by the FIA.

THE EFFECTS OF RACING DRIVING ON THE BODY

NECK
A car's tendency to lift over bumps can result in bad muscle strain.

COCCYX
The coccyx absorbs shocks caused by uneven track surfaces.

THUMBS
Thumbs can be dislocated by the steering wheel if curbs are taken at speed.

KNEES
The top of the fibula is especially prone to knocks in the cockpit.

EYES
Certain vibrations can hasten eye fatigue and lead to loss of attention.

ELBOWS
Elbows take a lot of bangs against the cockpit.

RIBS
Ribs can occasionally fracture as a result of driving over curbs.

FEET
Frequent heavy braking can cause painful soles.

CONCENTRATION

While not all drivers have perfect vision, their attention span is longer than average and their resistance to eye fatigue is high.

SOME DRIVERS WEAR GLASSES!

Formula 1 drivers are not supermen. Although their level of physical fitness is well above average, some do suffer from eyesight problems. Paul Belmondo and Ivan Capelli, for example, wore glasses under their helmet, as did Erik Comas, although in the Frenchman's case they were sunglasses, which he preferred to using a tinted visor.

The cockpit of a Formula 1 car

For something like 15 years, drivers have not been entirely alone in their cockpit since they have become assisted by computer aids in a number of fields. Yet while electronics have to a certain extent invaded Formula 1, the driver remains very much the sole master on board. Today's in-car systems are there solely either to detect a possible mechanical failure or to signal to the driver that he is not exploiting his material to maximum effect. For ease of accessibility and visibility at speeds of up to, and even exceeding, 300 km/h, all dials and switches are located immediately around the steering wheel. Meanwhile, Formula 1 is taking a growing interest in the science of economics.

FIGHTER PLANE
With its flashing lights, liquid crystal displays, switches, and multicolored buttons, it only needs a meteorological radar for the cockpit of a Formula 1 car to be mistaken for that of a plane! All these instruments have become essential tools for the modern driver who, to achieve the limit of his machine at all times, must be constantly informed about the performance of his chassis and engine. Thanks to the array of computerized displays and warning lights located around the steering wheel, the likes of Hill, Schumacher, or Alesi can progressively modify, if they wish, a number of parameters in their quest to improve lap times. Without these instruments, even the world's best drivers would, in a way, be half-blind.

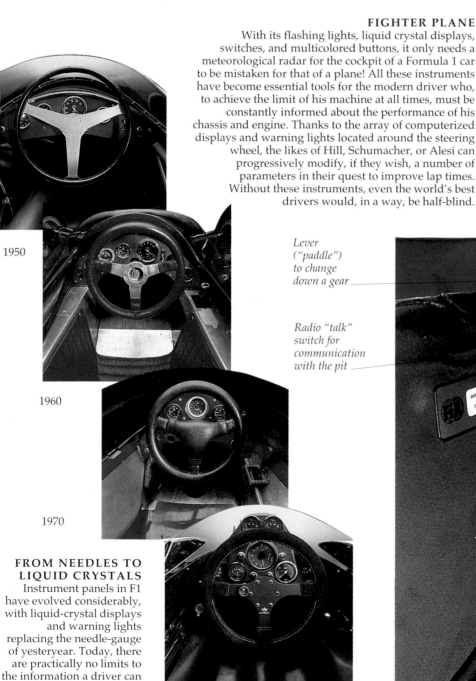

Engine cut switch

Neutral button

Lever ("paddle") to change down a gear

Radio "talk" switch for communication with the pit

1950

1960

1970

FROM NEEDLES TO LIQUID CRYSTALS
Instrument panels in F1 have evolved considerably, with liquid-crystal displays and warning lights replacing the needle-gauge of yesteryear. Today, there are practically no limits to the information a driver can have at his fingertips.

1980

TAILOR-MADE DISCOMFORT
Seats are molded to the exact dimensions of drivers' bodies. Totally devoid of any sort of padding, their sole function is to hold the driver firmly inside the cockpit.

SEAT
Molded directly around the driver's back, the two carbon shells are assembled together before being trimmed with leather. This helps prevent the body from sliding in the seat.

LIQUID-CRYSTAL DISPLAY OF A
WILLIAMS-RENAULT FW17

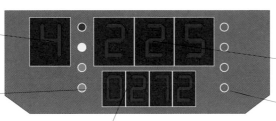

Current gear ratio (in this case 4th). In the event of a problem, the letter "F" (for fault) is displayed

Engine revs (green, then yellow, then red as max revs are reached

Multipurpose button for saving chassis and engine data onto onboard computer. Also drink button during race and pit lane speed limiter when in 2nd gear

Auxiliary display (selectable) usually shows speed-trap time (272 km/h) or sector time.

Main display (selectable) usually shows last lap time. Here it reads 1 min 22.5 secs.

Warning lights (selectable) can be programmed by engineers to warn driver of abnormal water or oil temperatures/pressures.

System warning light

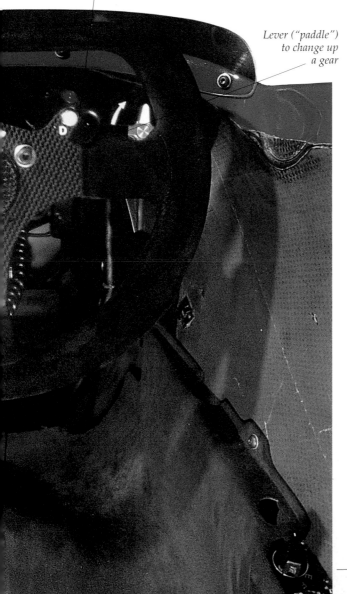

Lever ("paddle") to change up a gear

Fire extinguisher

Transmission isolate switch

Oil pump switch

Fuel pump warning light

Brake balance adjuster

Main power switch

Rear light on – obligatory in rain

Throttle sensitivity adjuster

Air/fuel mixture adjustment

High/low rev limit adjuster

Liquid-crystal display keeps driver informed (see detail)

Transmission strategy

Setting up a Formula 1 car

To be 100% competitive, a Formula 1 car must be carefully adjusted – or "set up" – to suit the characteristics of the circuit on which it is to race. Every time a new track is visited, or each time weather conditions change, settings are revised. Previous experience of a circuit, data recorded during previous seasons, or computer simulations enable a certain amount of work to be prepared in advance back at base. However, fine-tuning is always necessary once at the circuit. Setting up a car is a long and difficult job. The permutations possible are practically limitless and nearly all engine and chassis components are adjustable to match the specific demands of each track. The principal difficulty lies in identifying what adjustments are required to cure a given problem. This is where experienced racers can often have the edge over newcomers.

REAR WING
Rear downforce can be modified by adjusting the angle and/or dimensions of the rear wing.

TIRE PRESSURE
For optimum grip, the tires must be at their ideal working temperature, which is influenced by tire pressure.

TRANSMISSION
Gearing should be selected in response to the circuit's characteristics.

ENGINE
The engine's electronic control unit (ECU) looks after its own settings and automatically modifies them as a function of parameters such as atmospheric pressure and ambient humidity. Drivers can nonetheless adjust the richness of the air/fuel mixture being injected into the combustion chambers directly from the cockpit.

GROUND CLEARANCE
A car's ground clearance can affect its balance (understeer or oversteer) and can be adjusted by modifying the length of the pull-rods.

BALANCE
Causes of understeer or oversteer can be very simple – a driver turning in too late for a corner, for example, or accelerating too early out of it. Sometimes, however, the reason can be more complicated and can arise from a poor setup. Insufficient downforce at the front or rear, low grip as a result of under-inflated tires, or an incorrectly adjusted differential can result in mediocre overall balance.

Understeer

Neutral handling

Oversteer

EVERYTHING ON A FORMULA 1 CAR IS ADJUSTABLE
From steering wheel to engine, from pedals to the angle of the wheels, from ground clearance to aerodynamics, the majority of parts on a Formula 1 car are adjustable. And those that aren't can be replaced! As a general rule, during a test session, a driver will go out for three laps at a time, stopping at his pits between each series to talk with his engineer. All adjustments are carefully noted and, after the session, findings are compared with telemetry data-printouts.

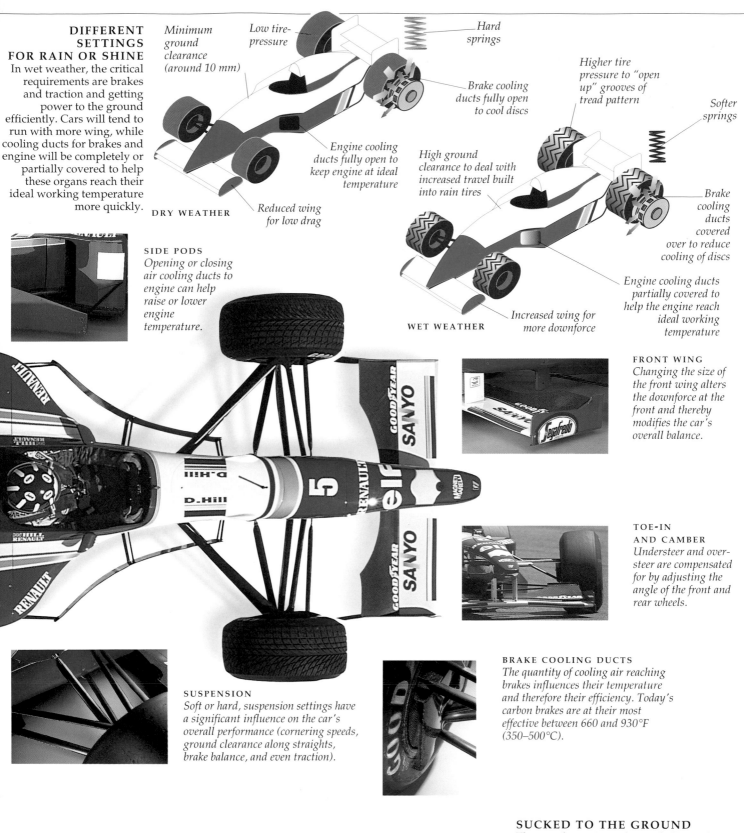

DIFFERENT SETTINGS FOR RAIN OR SHINE

In wet weather, the critical requirements are brakes and traction and getting power to the ground efficiently. Cars will tend to run with more wing, while cooling ducts for brakes and engine will be completely or partially covered to help these organs reach their ideal working temperature more quickly.

Minimum ground clearance (around 10 mm)

Low tire-pressure

Hard springs

Brake cooling ducts fully open to cool discs

Higher tire pressure to "open up" grooves of tread pattern

Softer springs

Engine cooling ducts fully open to keep engine at ideal temperature

High ground clearance to deal with increased travel built into rain tires

Brake cooling ducts covered over to reduce cooling of discs

DRY WEATHER

Reduced wing for low drag

WET WEATHER

Increased wing for more downforce

Engine cooling ducts partially covered to help the engine reach ideal working temperature

SIDE PODS
Opening or closing air cooling ducts to engine can help raise or lower engine temperature.

FRONT WING
Changing the size of the front wing alters the downforce at the front and thereby modifies the car's overall balance.

TOE-IN AND CAMBER
Understeer and oversteer are compensated for by adjusting the angle of the front and rear wheels.

SUSPENSION
Soft or hard, suspension settings have a significant influence on the car's overall performance (cornering speeds, ground clearance along straights, brake balance, and even traction).

BRAKE COOLING DUCTS
The quantity of cooling air reaching brakes influences their temperature and therefore their efficiency. Today's carbon brakes are at their most effective between 660 and 930°F (350–500°C).

STREAMLINED AND ECONOMICAL
The performance of a sedan such as the Safrane depends on the fluidity of its lines. Effective streamlining helps reduce fuel consumption.

HIGH DRAG COEFFICIENT
The "open-wheel" design and down-forcing wings of a Formula 1 car cause its drag coefficient to be inferior to that of the Safrane.

SUCKED TO THE GROUND

The aerodynamic qualities of a Formula 1 car enable it to take corners at high speed because the front and rear wings help keep it "glued" to the ground. Wings can be adjusted by changing their angle or by adding counter flaps at each end. The suction effect, generated by a combination of downforce and a zone of low pressure created underneath the car as it travels at speeds of up to 300 km/h, means it could – theoretically – be driven across a ceiling.

Driving techniques

A FORMULA 1 CAR IS A BRUTISH MONSTER that needs handling with great caution. Just keeping it in a straight line with something in the order of 700 bhp strapped to your back is a highly delicate exercise. The slightest error and you're into a spin, or even off the track. Drivers who make it into Formula 1 generally have at least ten years of racing experience behind them. Whatever their car, the basic techniques of competition driving – such as position of hands, footwork, and braking points – are the same as when they set out in the sport.

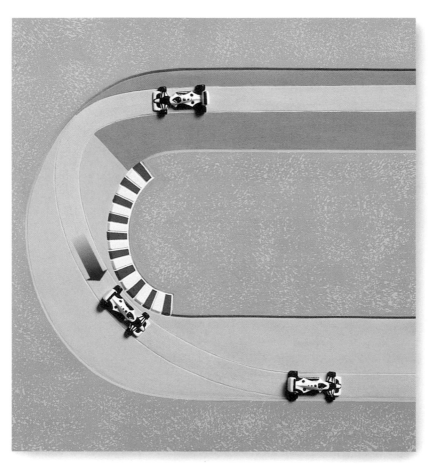

FAST CORNERS
In order to lose a minimum of speed through two consecutive fast corners, drivers look for the straightest line between the two, passing from apex to apex to get in line and reaccelerate as early as possible.

HAIRPINS
Drivers brake in a straight line (red zone) before turning-in late at the outside of the corner. Entry into the corner is sacrificed in order to have as straight a line as possible out of it and therefore to be in a position to reaccelerate very early.

S-BENDS
In this case, the first corner is tighter than the second. A driver will brake before the apex of the first (red zone) and, as soon as he turns in, he will aim for the following apex to "open out" the next corner. He can reaccelerate as soon as he has finished braking for the first corner.

HANDS ON THE WHEEL
Only half a turn is required to go from lock to lock and drivers need never take their hands off the steering wheel. Even for the tightest of hairpins, simply crossing the wrists is sufficient to be at maximum lock.

Along straights, hands should be positioned at "quarter-to-three."

Through fast corners, the inside hand "pulls" the wheel.

Arms might cross to achieve full lock through a hairpin.

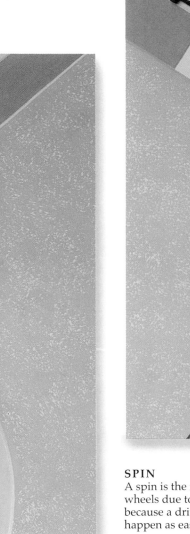

SPIN
A spin is the result of a sudden loss of grip of the rear wheels due to a poor racing line, excessive speed, or because a driver has reaccelerated too hard. A spin can happen as easily at 50 km/h as it can at 250 km/h.

CHICANES
Generally added with a view to slowing speeds along a fast straight, chicanes must be tackled with extreme caution. Number one priority is to maintain as much momentum as possible. Drivers must therefore try to keep the straightest line possible and keep movement of the steering wheel to a minimum.

DOUBLE-DECLUTCHING
Earlier Formula 1 cars had no synchromesh, so drivers had to double-declutch, blipping the throttle with the car in neutral before changing down a gear.

HILL: SMOOTH
Damon Hill prefers a relatively upright driving position and his lines are always very smooth and precise. He doesn't fight the car. In this way, he is often able to complete three flying laps per set of tires during qualifying practice.

ALESI: ATTACK
Jean Alesi places his hands high on the steering wheel and drives with his head bent forward, almost as though he wants to eat up the track. He brakes very late and accelerates early, always sliding, always on the attack. Without doubt the most spectacular driver in Formula 1 today.

SCHUMACHER: TRUE GRIT
Fast corners are his speciality and are where he probably has the edge over his rivals. His secret? Permanent control of his car's balance using the throttle.

Electronics in Formula 1

In 1989, FORMULA 1 became aware of what electronics could do for performance. Features such as active suspension, traction control, antilocking brakes, and automatic transmissions saw computers take on increasing importance alongside the driver in the cockpit and become more and more the key to success. At the end of 1993, with a view to placing the emphasis once again on driver skill, the FIA took the decision to outlaw many of these aids. Electronics are now rarely employed for anything other than engine management and telemetry.

ELECTRONIC ENGINE MANAGEMENT
Electronic calculators take account of ambient air temperature, atmospheric pressure, and other functional parameters as they make constant fuel richness, injection, and ignition adjustments.

POWER THROTTLE
The familiar steel throttle cable not only takes up space but also has a tendency to stretch or break. Today, it is increasingly an electrical signal that transmits instructions from the pedal to the engine, a system that enables acceleration to be controlled more progressively.

SEMIAUTOMATIC TRANSMISSION
Drivers no longer take their hands from the steering wheel to change gear, but just activate two small levers with their finger tips. The clutch is only used to engage first gear when moving off.

1989: NEAR-REVOLUTION IN TRANSMISSION TECHNOLOGY

The 1989 Brazilian Grand Prix will be remembered in the history of Formula 1 as the first race to be won by a car fitted with a semiautomatic transmission. Using a system devised by John Barnard, Nigel Mansell did not need to take his hands off the wheel at any stage of the race. Moving up and down the gears became a simple matter of flicking one of two switches located to the left and right on the reverse side of the steering wheel.

This electrohydraulic system was soon taken up by all the top teams, including Williams-Renault, Benetton-Renault, and McLaren.

AN ELECTRONIC STETHOSCOPE
Thanks to dozens of sensors located at strategic points in the car, data is transmitted to the pits either in real time or each time it passes the pits, enabling engineers to keep a constant watch on the chassis and engine.

KEEPING TABS
Engine telemetry keeps a permanent watch on 50 or so pressure- and temperature-related parameters that are relayed by radio to computers in the pits each time the car passes by. The system enables specialized engineers to keep a lap-by-lap "bill of health" of their block.

ELECTRONIC AIDS
Four "driver aids," which contribute either to performance or ensuring that all is running smoothly, are authorized by the regulations.

TELEMETRY
Thanks to sensors located at strategic points around the car, telemetry keeps a constant track of selected engine and chassis parameters. Technicians download data either by radio or by floppy disks.

Safety in Formula 1

Sɪɴᴄᴇ 1950, ᴛʜᴇ ᴘᴇʀꜰᴏʀᴍᴀɴᴄᴇ of Formula 1 cars has never ceased to increase. Thanks to new technologies and materials derived from the aeronautical industry, cars are not only quicker but also corner faster and brake later. Their resistance to impact has also improved over the years, to the extent that drivers admit to feeling invulnerable in case of an accident. However, the fatal crashes of Roland Ratzenberger and Ayrton Senna in 1994, followed by Karl Wendlinger's serious accident, brought them cruelly back to reality: despite progress in the realm of safety, Formula 1 is an extremely dangerous sport and the recent series of tragedies resulted in a veritable revolution in the regulations. Indeed, from the strengthening of tubs to enhanced driver protection, safety has – justifiably – become an obsession for the Formula 1 Driver's Association and for the International Federation.

The rollover bar prevents drivers being squashed in the event of a roll.

Full-harness belts restrain the driver and prevent him from being ejected.

CRASHES

Should a driver lose control of his machine, it is preferable to try to swipe any obstacle sideways, or with the rear. The car can absorb energy more efficiently in this way. In case of frontal impact, drivers try to fold up their legs and crouch over in their seat. During the 1989 French Grand Prix, Mauricio Gugelmin had little time to think when a rival car climbed his rear wheel. The Brazilian happily escaped unhurt from the ensuing spectacular crash, and he was ready for the race's restart.

NUMBER OF
DRIVERS KILLED
EACH DECADE

1950–59: 21

1960–69: 27

1970–79: 12

1980–89: 7

1990–95: 2

SEE AND BE SEEN
In the case of poor visibility, drivers must switch
on a red light fitted at the rear of the car.

*In case of fire, an onboard
oxygen bottle ensures
roughly thirty seconds
supply of breathable air.
Very few drivers actually
connect this system to
their helmet.*

SURVIVAL KIT
Driver safety is paramount,
and a battery of mandatory
FIA-approved equipment
guarantees that drivers are
afforded maximum protection
in the event of a collision or fire.
Scrutineers regularly check to
see that this equipment is on
board the cars.

*To reduce the risk of fire, Formula 1
cars use deformable fuel tanks made
from puncture-proof Kevlar. All fuel
lines are of the auto cutoff type in case
of breakage and an extinguisher is
plumbed into this "sensitive" zone
of the car.*

FORMULA 1
SAMARITANS
Ambulances and fire-
fighting vehicles are
located at strategic
points around the
circuit in order to be in
action within seconds
of any accident.

Official practice

DRIVERS SPEND practically the entire two days of official practice in conversation with their Team Director, engineers, mechanics, sponsors, or journalists. Curiously, they spend precious little time in their cars, especially since new regulations introduced in 1993 set an upper limit on the number of laps each driver is able to complete (30 laps in free practice on Friday and Saturday, 12 in qualifying practice on Saturday). On average, a driver will spend just one hour actually driving his car on each of the two days of practice. On the other hand, in the privacy of his pits or motorhome, he will spend more than six hours a day in technical meetings in an effort to find the ideal settings.

STARTING GRID
Official practice takes place on the Friday and Saturday before every Grand Prix, except in Monaco where first qualifying takes place on the Thursday. The timetable is always identical: free practice 11:00–12:00 and 13:00–14:00 on Friday, and then 09.30-10.15 and 10:30–11:15 on Saturday; qualifying practice from 13:00-14:00 on Saturday. The best lap times in qualifying practice determine the starting grid positions for Sunday's race. The only drivers to qualify are those whose lap time is within 7% of the best time.

6 : Herbert,
Benetton-Renault
1 min 28.498 secs

5 : Alesi, Ferrari
1 min 28.474 secs

4 : Berger, Ferrari
1 min 28.189 secs

1995 CANADIAN GRAND PRIX

3 : Coulthard,
Williams-Renault
1 min 28.091 secs

2 : Hill,
Williams-Renault
1 min 28.039 secs

1 : Schumacher,
Benetton-Renault
1 min 27.661 secs

CHANGING ROOM
Drivers change into racing overalls in the team's transporter. Gloves and helmet will be put on just before climbing into the car. As a general rule, drivers leave transportation of gear such as overalls, shoes, and gloves to the team.

A DAY IN THE LIFE
The schedule for practice follows the same routine at every race. Whatever the circuit, drivers always observe the same ritual, arriving at the track, eating lunch, and holding technical briefings at the same time each day. Every minute is committed to improving the car's performance.

BASIC SETTINGS
When the driver is ready, he discusses with the engineers the car's basic settings, selected according to the type of circuit. A program of work is established for the free practice session.

ARRIVAL AT THE CIRCUIT
Drivers get to the circuit at about 8 am. If the team has the means, and if traffic is congested, they might arrive by helicopter. More usually however, they arrive by car. A special parking lot is provided for them close to the paddock.

AUTOGRAPH HUNTERS
Entry to the paddock is strictly controlled. However, determined spectators occasionally succeed in slipping through the net. They are willing to wait for hours by the gate in the hope of getting an autograph.

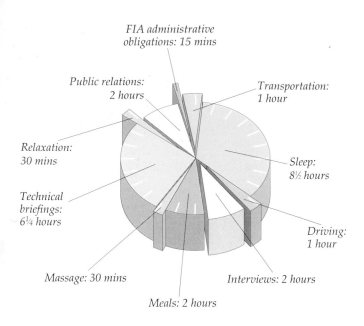

FIA administrative
obligations: 15 mins

Public relations:
2 hours

Transportation:
1 hour

Relaxation:
30 mins

Sleep:
8½ hours

Technical
briefings:
6¼ hours

Massage: 30 mins

Driving:
1 hour

Interviews: 2 hours

Meals: 2 hours

INTERVIEWS
Approximately 600 media representatives attend each Grand Prix, and drivers will spend an average of two hours every day with journalists. This can take the form of individual interviews or press conferences. The drivers most in demand, of course, are those who set the best qualifying times.

24 HOURS IN THE LIFE OF A FORMULA 1 DRIVER
About six hours are spent discussing the setting up of the car, compared with just 2½ hours on the track. This may seem disproportionate, but such meetings can have an important bearing on the final outcome of the race.

THE MEDIA
Practice has just finished and, after climbing out of his car, Damon Hill is surrounded by the press. As a general rule, he will give them a few minutes of his time before sitting down to a light lunch with his team and engineers.

QUALIFYING PRACTICE
Drivers have one hour, 12 laps, and two sets of tires to try to set the fastest lap time possible.

THREE RUNS
Damon Hill returns to his pits after his first run (out lap, two flying laps, and in lap) to fine-tune settings and to catch up on how his rivals are faring by means of a timing monitor placed on his car by mechanics. At the same time, they will also be looking for a moment when the track is relatively free of "traffic" to go out for a second or third run.

POLE POSITION
Damon Hill has just set the fastest time of the day and will therefore start the next day's race from pole position, the most coveted place on the grid. His performance also means additional work: the fastest driver in practice must go directly to the media room for a press conference before being able to return to his motorhome for a debriefing session with his engineers.

TEAM DISCUSSION
After lunch, between free practice and qualifying practice, drivers have less than two hours at their disposal to reflect on the best settings for their cars.

FREE PRACTICE (1½ HOURS)
Drivers have a maximum of 23 laps during Friday and Saturday's free practice (1½ hours) to set up their cars with full fuel tanks. They will also test with empty tanks in order to have the best chance of setting a blistering lap time during the afternoon's qualifying session.

MOTORHOMES
Each team has its own luxury motorhome in the paddock. This is where drivers retire to eat or be massaged, while Team Directors profit from its privacy to entertain VIP guests or negotiate future contracts. It is also here that mechanics will take their evening meal at the end of the day when all at the circuit is calm.

The media and Formula 1

FORMULA 1 IS ONE OF THE SPORTS that generate the greatest amount of media coverage in the world. The number of journalists following F1 – barely a handful in 1950 when the World Championship was created – has literally gone through the ceiling. Today, the sport is covered by something like 6,000 reporters representing 40 different countries and all types of media. Beforehand, however, they must have applied for special authorization from the FIA to obtain the necessary access passes into circuits. TV companies must pay special broadcasting rights.

TRULY INTERNATIONAL
In the press office of a Formula 1 Grand Prix, you are likely to hear nearly every language spoken in the world. Journalists begin to arrive at the circuit on the Thursday prior to the first day of official practice. Facilities at their disposal include full television coverage of the race, as well as monitors providing lap-by-lap times and overall positions.

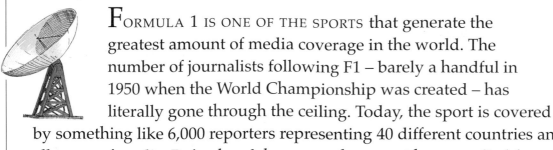

PRESS CONFERENCES
To simplify the media's task, official press conferences provide an opportunity to question the drivers in the top three positions on the Saturday afternoon and, minutes after the flag on the Sunday, the top three finishers of the Grand Prix itself.

TV reporter

GLOBAL TV COVERAGE
Live satellite transmission of races has turned Formula 1 into a truly global sport covering all five continents. A total audience of 30 billion viewers is estimated to have followed the 1995 World Championship from their armchairs. Broadcasting rights are the property of the Formula 1 Constructors' Association (FOCA), which handles their sale to individual TV companies. No professional cameraman is able to gain access to a circuit unless his camera sports the special sticker certifying that he has already obtained the necessary authorization to film.

Cameraman

GOOD YEAR

SANYO

HUNGRY FOR INFORMATION

On the grid, during the minutes leading up to the start, it is easy to spot the most popular drivers by the number of reporters standing by their cars. These journalists wait to record the last-minute thoughts and quotes of the stars at the front of the grid.

NUMBER OF
JOURNALISTS
ACCREDITED FOR
SELECTED TOP
SPORTING EVENTS

Soccer World Cup: 7,000

A season of Formula 1: 6,000

America's Cup: 2,200

Roland Garros: 1,200

Tour de France: 900

Television sound engineer

Radio reporter

Reporter

JOURNALISTS IN THEIR THOUSANDS

Formula 1 is one of the sports that receive the most media coverage in the world. In 1995, no less than 6,000 photographers and newspaper, radio, and TV correspondents were accredited by the Fédération Internationale de l'Automobile to cover the F1 World Championship.

TONS OF PAPER

Each Grand Prix generates a huge amount of written information. On the photo front, in order to meet tight deadlines, certain magazines supply their photographers with special machines that analyze photos numerically. These pictures, like written articles, can then be transmitted directly to editorial desks around the world by telephone.

SHOOTING FILM

An average of 200 photographers are present at any one Grand Prix. In the space of three days, they will take something like 1,000 frames each, often processing them on-site before electronically transmitting them across the globe.

A Grand Prix start

T HE SECONDS IMMEDIATELY before the start, as cars take up position on the grid after the formation lap, are the most intense moment of a Grand Prix. Despite the clamor of the engines, all seems silent, a silence that only serves to accentuate the thunderous climax of the start itself. The two drivers on the front row have clear asphalt ahead. In the distance, they see the first corner, the first braking point. Those behind see just an abstract mass of tires and rear wings. It is through this wall that they must attempt to pick out a path when the green light comes on, even if that means wheel-to-wheel contact with other cars.

CONCENTRATION
Drivers' reactions when the light switches to green are on a par with those of a 100-meter sprinter as the starting pistol is fired – something in the order of a few hundredths of a second! The instant a driver lowers his visor, his thoughts are already elsewhere. Nothing else exists. The race has already begun.

INCREASING HEARTBEAT
A driver's heartbeat underlines how intense the start is. From 50 beats a minute, the figure rockets to 150, braking for the first corner.

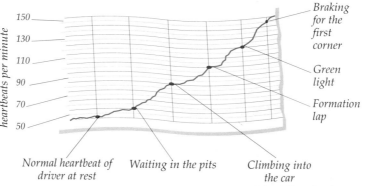

heartbeats per minute

150
130
110
90
70
50

Braking for the first corner

Green light

Formation lap

Normal heartbeat of driver at rest   *Waiting in the pits*   *Climbing into the car*

The reward for being fastest in qualifying practice is pole position, the inside slot on the front row

THE STARTING GRID
From first to last, the position of drivers on the grid is a function of the best personal time set during qualifying practice on Saturday. A painted mark indicates the spot where cars should stop. To reduce the risk of tangles, the grid is staggered and two cars on the same row are separated by a distance of four meters. An eight-meter gap separates cars lined up on either side of the track.

COUNTDOWN
Start procedure begins 30 minutes before the scheduled start as cars join the track for one or more reconnaissance laps. Those opting for more than one lap must pass via the pit lane at reduced speed each time. Once cars are in position on the grid, the countdown starts. Certain drivers stay in their cars, helmets on, motionless. Others prefer to stretch their legs and chat, helmets off. Progressively, the grid clears and engines fire up as the mechanics return to the pits. The drivers are on their own as they wait for the formation lap to start.

Formula 1 cars take to the track to complete a reconnaissance lap before taking up their place on the grid.

A siren announces that the pit lane has been closed. Any car remaining in its pits can still start the race, but from the back of the grid.

WHEELSPIN

Caused by accelerating too hard or letting out the clutch too briskly, wheelspin is what drivers dread the most as the light turns to green. Rear wheels, unable to transmit all the power effectively, spin helplessly. Drivers stand to lose a few places if this happens to them.

The green light flashes on and 26 drivers put their foot to the floor simultaneously. The Grand Prix has started.

THE MOMENT OF RISK

Drivers know perfectly well that the best chance of making up a few places is between the starting line and the moment cars start to brake for the first corner. Those in front generally succeed in squeezing through. Behind, however, wheel-to-wheel dicing and a tendency to bottleneck make this one of the riskiest moments of the entire race.

Yellow light: an incident – a stalled engine perhaps – has interrupted the start. A slow lap is completed before drivers take up position again.

When the red light shows, drivers know the start will be given within between four to seven seconds.

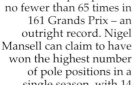

OTHER TYPES OF START

The traditional Le Mans start (left) involved drivers running across the track and jumping into their cars. Spectacular but unsafe. It was replaced in 1969 by a "rolling start" behind an official pace-car that dives to one side as it crosses the starting line. This system is also used in Indy racing (right).

Once all boards are lowered, the starter shows the 5-second board. The red light will come on within the next five seconds.

POLE POSITION

Ayrton Senna was the undisputed master when it came to qualifying. During his career, he started from pole position no fewer than 65 times in 161 Grands Prix – an outright record. Nigel Mansell can claim to have won the highest number of pole positions in a single season, with 14 poles in 1992, while Alain Prost took the highest number of consecutive poles (7) in 1993.

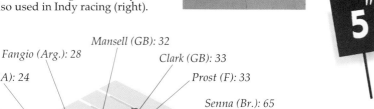

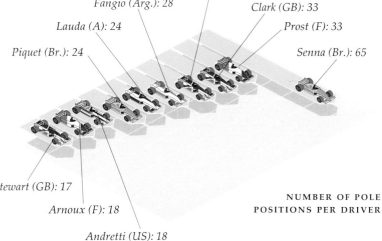

Mansell (GB): 32
Fangio (Arg.): 28
Clark (GB): 33
Lauda (A): 24
Prost (F): 33
Piquet (Br.): 24
Senna (Br.): 65
Stewart (GB): 17
Arnoux (F): 18
Andretti (US): 18

NUMBER OF POLE POSITIONS PER DRIVER

Cars pull up at their allotted place on the grid. As they do so, a marshal (one per car) lowers the flag bearing the driver's number.

N° 2

10'

The grid is cleared. Only the driver, his car, and his mechanics may remain.

1'

Engines start and it is now the mechanics' turn to leave the track.

30"

Within thirty seconds of this board being shown, a green flag at the front of the grid will wave cars off for the formation lap.

Cars set off for the formation lap before taking up position again on the grid, engines running.

The race

THE HIGHLIGHT of the Grand Prix weekend is, of course, the race. The instant the light turns green, 26 highly determined drivers are literally unleashed. For the driver in front, his immediate task is to build up his lead and ward off the pressure of his pursuers. For those caught up in the pack, the job is doubly difficult. Along every straight, through every corner, their sole objective is to carve a way through the field. Overtaking is the name of the game, moving up the leaderboard to finish in the highest position possible.

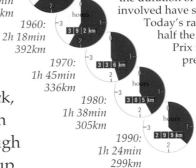

1950:
2h 40min
408km

1960:
2h 18min
392km

1970:
1h 45min
336km

1980:
1h 38min
305km

1990:
1h 24min
299km

SHORT AND ACTION-PACKED
Since the creation of Formula 1, both the duration of races and the distances involved have shortened considerably. Today's races last little more than half the time taken for a Grand Prix in the 1950s. TV, which prefers short, action-filled races, is the principal reason for this trend.

DURATION AND
LENGTH OF GRANDS
PRIX SINCE 1950

OVERTAKING TECHNIQUES

LATE BRAKING
The driver of the white car has out-braked his rival on the inside line. He is therefore able to turn in earlier and accelerate out of the corner in front. A textbook maneuver!

SLIPSTREAMING
The driver of the white car is less affected by aerodynamic turbulence. As he pulls out to overtake, he benefits from an added turn of speed to pass and pull clear.

OVERTAKING AT MONZA AND MONACO
Racing is all about overtaking. Unfortunately, the layout of certain circuits can make this a very complicated task indeed. The ideal place is at the end of a long straight preceding a reasonably tight corner. This gives the braver drivers a chance to out-brake their rivals. Monza boasts a number of such places. At the other end of the scale, the absence of straights around Monaco's narrow, cambered street-circuit makes overtaking all but impossible. An eloquent example was Mansell's duel with Senna there in 1992. Despite being four seconds a lap quicker, the British driver eventually had to give up trying to pass and settle for second.

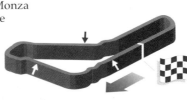

Monza

Monaco

THE MOST GRAND PRIX STARTS (TEAMS)

Ferrari
554
Grands Prix

Lotus
490

McLaren
427

Brabham
394

Tyrrell
369

Williams
346

Ligier
310

Arrows
272

March
230

B.R.M.
197

THE MOST GRAND PRIX STARTS (DRIVERS)

Patrese (I)
256 Grands Prix

De Cesaris
(I)
208

Piquet (Br.)
204

Prost
(F)
199

Alboreto (I)
194

Mansell
(GB)
187

Berger (A)
180

G. Hill
(GB)
176

Laffite (F)
176

Lauda
(A)
171

DRINKING AND DRIVING
Some drivers carry water with them. The liquid is held in a container fixed inside the cockpit, in the side pods, in the car's nose, or sometimes strapped to the pilot's chest. The pilot drinks by sucking or by means of a mini electric pump.

Schumacher recognizes his pit board by his helmet.

P1 indicates "first position" in the race.

Driver can come in for fuel when he wishes.

GETTING THE MESSAGE
The quality of radio contact with drivers is not always crystal sharp. Pit boards are therefore used to confirm important messages each time a driver passes his pit. In this example, the Benetton-Renault team informs Schumacher that he is leading the Grand Prix (P1), that he should stop at his pits for fuel (FUEL IN) and that there remain 32 laps of the race to be completed.

P1

FUEL IN

L32

L32 means there are 32 laps left

Pit stops

In 1994, THE REGULATIONS were modified to allow refueling in addition to the already familiar mid-race tire changes. The combination of the two means that pit stops must be perfectly synchronized in order to keep time loss to a minimum, and also, more importantly, to reduce the risks involved: a single drop of gasoline on the white-hot exhausts and the team can find itself with a fire on its hands. Dressed like astronauts, mechanics regularly rehearse pit stop procedure to ensure that the operation goes as smoothly as possible during the race. A successful stop can even allow a driver to make up a place or two on the leaderboard.

ALL FOR ONE

A pit stop requires 17 mechanics – three to remove and replace each wheel (one to unscrew and then tighten the nut, another to remove the original wheel and a third to position the new one), two to operate the front and rear quick-lift jacks, two to refuel plus the chief mechanic who holds the "lollipop." These may be joined by an assistant refueler, an engine technician, and two mechanics whose respective tasks are to clean the driver's visor and to remove papers or foreign bodies from side-pod air intakes to ensure optimal radiator efficiency.

SPARE TOOLS
In case of a problem, spare air guns are positioned around the car within easy reach of mechanics. Each crew also has a spare wheelnut in case the one on the car proves too damaged for reuse, a reasonably frequent occurrence.

THE CAR ARRIVES
Advised by his engineer that all is ready for the pit stop, the driver returns to his pits where he stops just in front of the front quick-lift jack.

THE TIRE CHANGE
The driver keeps his foot on the brake pedal as the front and rear jacks are lifted. Meanwhile, the original wheels are removed and thrown back into the pits before fresh tires are fitted.

A RISK OF THE JOB
Despite the fact that gloves are worn for wheel changes, it is not uncommon for mechanics to slightly burn their hands by accidentally touching the brake calipers, wheels, or tires – all of which are at their maximum temperature.

REFLEX WORK
Prior to the return of refueling, mid-race tire changes were lightning quick, race-against-the-clock affairs. A successful change lasted less than six seconds, a poor change could last twice that time, which meant that a skillful crew was potentially worth precious seconds to its drivers. Since 1994, however, refueling has to an extent taken the spice out of tire pit stops inasmuch as it is the time required to inject fuel into the tank which tends to dictate the duration of a stop. The time necessary to pump in fuel cannot be compressed.

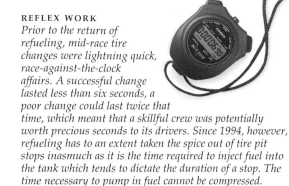

TIRE-CHANGE TIMES 1993 BRITISH GRAND PRIX								
1	2	3	4	5	6	7	8	9

McLaren: 5.11s (Senna)
Benetton: 5.50s (Schumacher)
Ligier: 6.75s (Brundle)
Williams: 7.61s (Hill)
Williams: 8.02s (Prost)
Lotus: 9.21s (Zanardi)

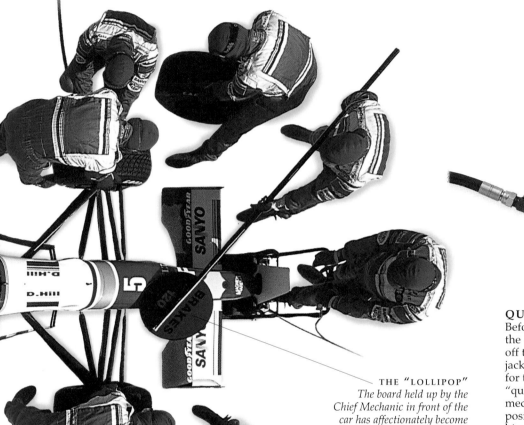

AIR POWER: THE ULTIMATE WEAPON
The wheels of Formula 1 cars are tightened with a single central wheelnut. To unscrew it and retighten it after a change, mechanics use air tools powered by bottles of compressed air located in the pits.

QUICK-LIFT JACKS
Before tires can be changed, the car first needs to be lifted off the ground. A mechanical jack would be far too slow for this job. Instead, a "quick-lift" jack is used. The mechanic wheels it into position before applying all his weight to the other end to lift the car. At the front, some teams prefer air-jacks, which are quicker and give drivers a better idea of the exact spot where they should stop.

THE "LOLLIPOP"
The board held up by the Chief Mechanic in front of the car has affectionately become known as the "lollipop." It either informs the driver that he must keep his foot on the brakes ("Brakes on") or that he is free to drive off ("Go").

REFUELING
The tires have been changed and the car is back on the ground as pressurized fuel continues to be pumped into the tank at a rate of 9 liters per second.

THE CAR LEAVES
The refueling hose is pulled clear and the chief mechanic pulls the "lollipop" clear. As the driver rejoins the race, the team has already started to prepare for the second car's pit stop.

Forced out

Being forced to retire from a race is probably the worst form of defeat for a driver, since it means he is unable to defend his chances right up to the flag. Over the years, technological progress has tended to reduce the proportion of retirements due to mechanical failures. However, the number of "driver-related" retirements, such as collisions or going off the track, is on the increase. Not that today's drivers are any less skillful. It's simply that cars are now so close in terms of performance, and braking distances have become so short, that drivers must take more risks if they want to move up a notch in practice or during a race.

SPIN
Spins are caused by a sudden loss of grip of the rear wheels, due either to braking too late or accelerating too early. A spin does not necessarily spell retirement from a race, unless the engine stalls, or the car ends up stranded in a sand trap.

HOW THE RELIABILITY OF FORMULA 1 CARS HAS EVOLVED

There are more retirements in F1 today than in the 1960s and 70s. However, there are fewer mechanical failures, while collisions and accidents are on the increase.

CAUSES OF RETIREMENT

Miscellaneous: 16 (7%)

Electrical or electronic failures: 14 (7%)

Spins and offs: 31 (14%)

Transmission: 33 (15%)

1994: 413 starts, 214 retirements

Engine: 57 (27%)

Collisions: 63 (30%)

Collisions and "offs" today account for 44% of all retirements in F1. The same figure in 1960, when engine and transmission failures were each responsible for a third of retirements, was 15%.

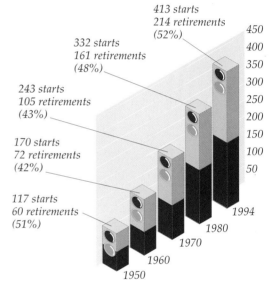

413 starts
214 retirements
(52%)

332 starts
161 retirements
(48%)

243 starts
105 retirements
(43%)

170 starts
72 retirements
(42%)

117 starts
60 retirements
(51%)

1950 1960 1970 1980 1994

COLLISIONS: WHOSE FAULT IS IT?

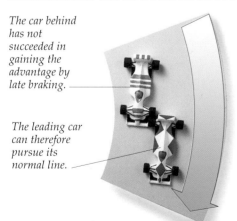

The car behind has not succeeded in gaining the advantage by late braking.

The leading car can therefore pursue its normal line.

The front wheels of the chasing car tangle with the rear wheels of the car in front.

Blame in this case is considered to be shared since neither driver wanted to back off.

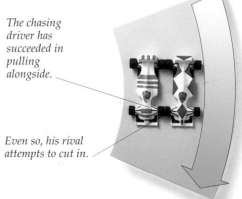

The chasing driver has succeeded in pulling alongside.

Even so, his rival attempts to cut in.

THE ASSAILANT IN THE WRONG
The second car tries to pass on the inside but hasn't gained sufficient advantage by braking late. The front car has every right to continue on its ideal line. However, the front wheel of the second car touches the rear wheel of the first car. The assailant is in the wrong. He should have backed off.

SHARED RESPONSIBILITY
The second car has stolen half a length by out-braking his rival. Although on the inside, he still hasn't enough lead to turn in first. The front car keeps to its ideal line. As neither is prepared to back off, responsibility is considered shared.

THE DEFENDER IN THE WRONG
Here, the chasing driver draws level with his rival under braking as they prepare to turn in. Since he is on the inside, he is well placed to steer into the corner first. However, the leading driver refuses to give way, and front and rear wheels touch. The driver trying to defend his position is in the wrong.

ELECTRICAL FAILURE

"Electrical failures" sometimes provide a handy excuse when a team either doesn't know the real reason for a problem or else doesn't want it to be known. Even so, a severed wire, a faulty coil, a malfunction on one of the electronic management packs, or an alternator failure can effectively cause an engine to stop.

CLUTCH

A poor start or a spin might lead a driver to ask too much of his clutch. Excessive clutch slip causes the carbon clutch plate to overheat and this in turn can result in the clutch hub's splines sheering off, spelling instant retirement.

TRANSMISSION

A return to reasonable levels of power has reduced the number of transmission failures, which used to be frequent in the days of the turbo. Considerable ongoing work goes into reducing the weight of the transmission, but gears and shift-forks do not always stand up to such slimming exercises.

ENGINE

Engine failure results from one of four reasons – a broken internal component, electronic failure, excessive oil consumption, or blocked side pods that cause overheating. The first is the most spectacular. The part that breaks very often puts a hole in the sump, and the consequent loss of oil causes a tremendous cloud of smoke. The advent of semiautomatic transmissions has all but eliminated engine failure caused by over-revving.

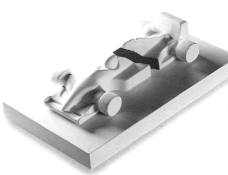

PUNCTURES

The usual cause of a puncture in Formula 1 is driving over debris – left on the track after a collision, for example. Air loss from the tire is slow, and drivers generally have sufficient time to reach their pits to fit fresh tires. A tire that is worn, however, can sometimes explode, and this means instant retirement. This is what happened to Damon Hill two laps from the finish of the 1993 German Grand Prix, when victory seemed in the bag.

COLLISIONS

While the reliability of Formula 1 cars continues to improve, the same cannot be said of drivers. Collisions, a rare occurrence in the 1950s and 60s, are today the most common cause of retirement. Excessive driver optimism is not the only reason for this. The growing number of collisions is a clear indication that overtaking, the whole point of racing, has become extremely difficult in Formula 1.

GOING OFF

In wet weather, grip is low and the number of spins and cars leaving the track tends to rise. Drivers generally don't like to admit it was their fault when they find themselves "parked" off the track. In their defense, mechanical problems or patches of oil not signaled by marshals are responsible for one-half of all accidents.

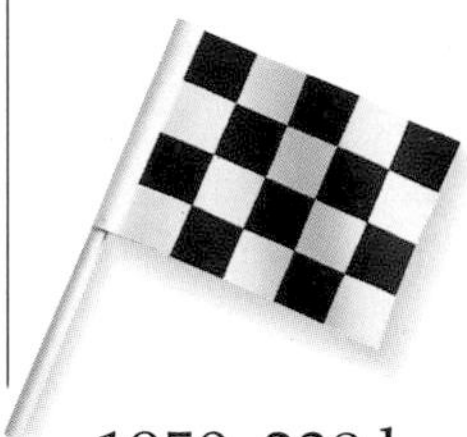

Victory!

OF THE 564 DRIVERS who have raced in F1 since 1950, 238 have scored World Championship points. Only 73 belong to the elite club of past Grand Prix winners, however, and of these, 19 can lay claim to no more than one success. Most of these one-off results can be explained either by a stroke of good fortune or because the drivers in question sadly lost their lives just as their careers were taking off. Musso, Bandini, Cevert, Nilsson, and Pace were in this latter category. Two drivers who amply deserved to win – but didn't – were New Zealander Chris Amon and France's Jean-Pierre Jarier. During his career, Amon covered a distance of nearly 800 km in front – the equivalent of three Grands Prix – without ever succeeding in being first across the line, often falling foul of some mechanical problem with the flag in sight. British driver Peter Gethin was more fortunate. In his entire career, he spent just 11 kilometers in front. That was enough for him to clinch the 1971 Italian Grand Prix by a margin of just 1/100th of a second.

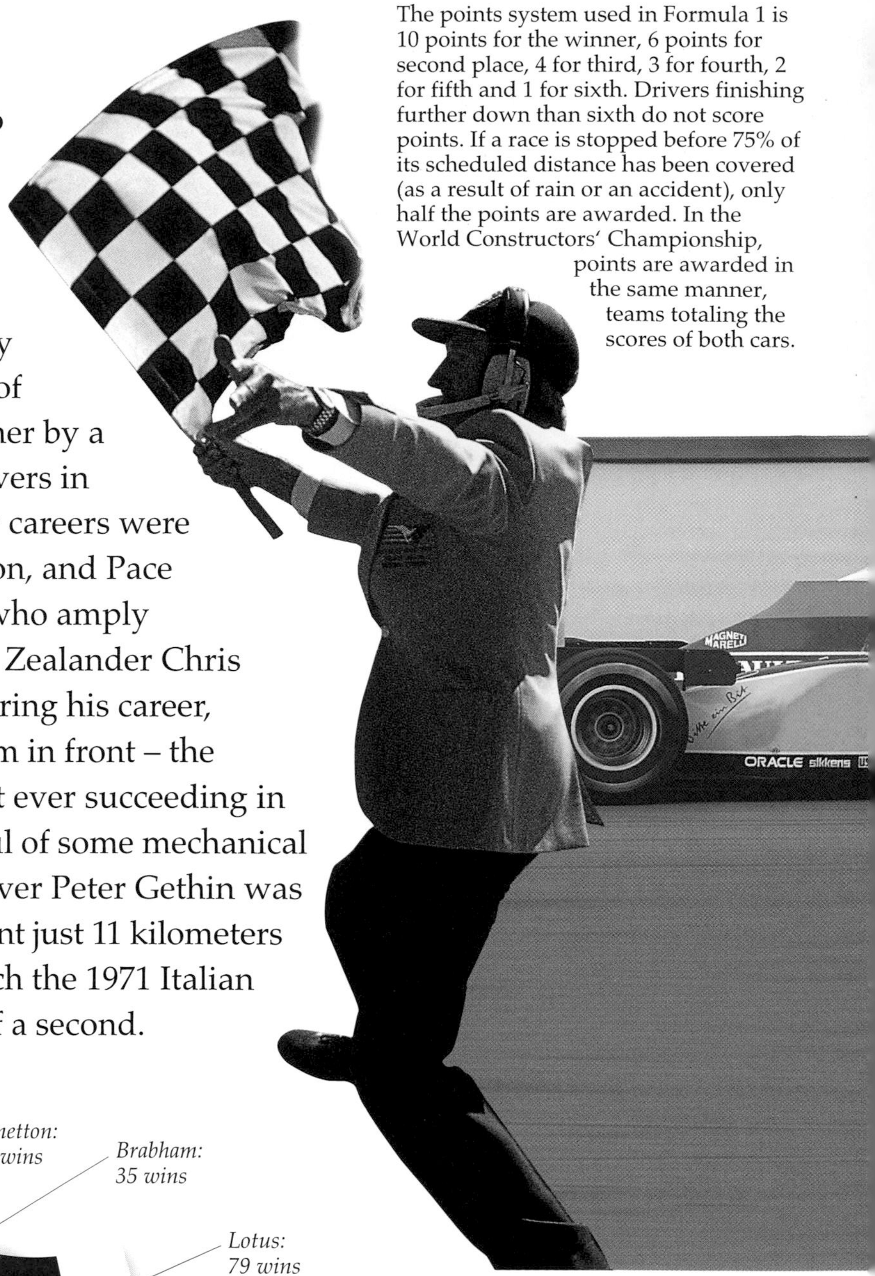
ORACLE sikkens

THE CHECKERED FLAG
The points system used in Formula 1 is 10 points for the winner, 6 points for second place, 4 for third, 3 for fourth, 2 for fifth and 1 for sixth. Drivers finishing further down than sixth do not score points. If a race is stopped before 75% of its scheduled distance has been covered (as a result of rain or an accident), only half the points are awarded. In the World Constructors' Championship, points are awarded in the same manner, teams totaling the scores of both cars.

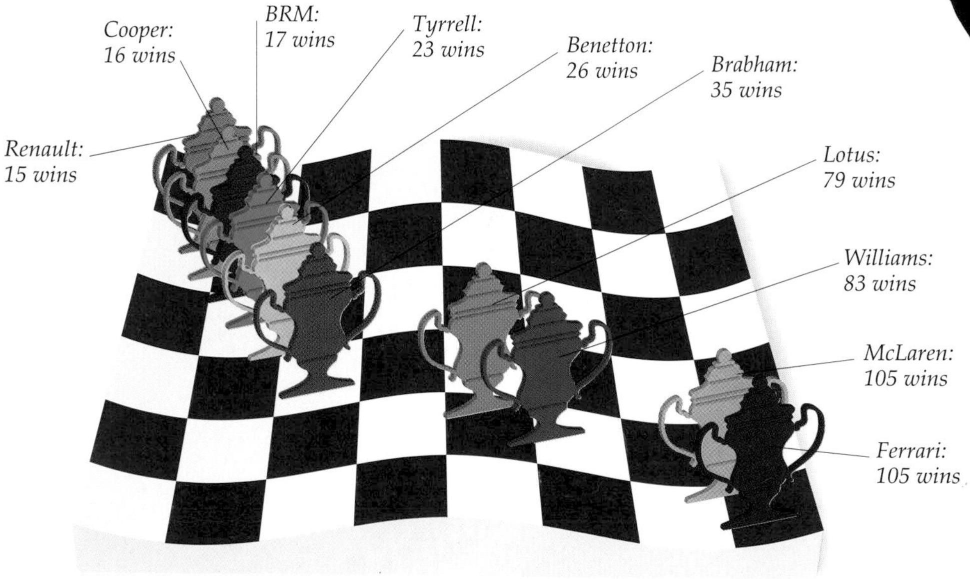
Cooper: 16 wins
BRM: 17 wins
Tyrrell: 23 wins
Benetton: 26 wins
Brabham: 35 wins
Renault: 15 wins
Lotus: 79 wins
Williams: 83 wins
McLaren: 105 wins
Ferrari: 105 wins

NUMBER OF WINS PER TEAM
Ferrari, the only team present in Formula 1 since the creation of the World Championship, holds the record for the highest number of Grand Prix wins. Having dominated the sport in the 1980s, McLaren has recently gone through a more barren phase, while Williams and Benetton have scored 42 of the 65 Grands Prix to have been organized since 1992.

PROST'S RECORD
With a total of 51 wins, Alain Prost holds the record for the most wins in F1. His most pressing challenger was Ayrton Senna but, tragically, fate did not leave the Brazilian sufficient time.

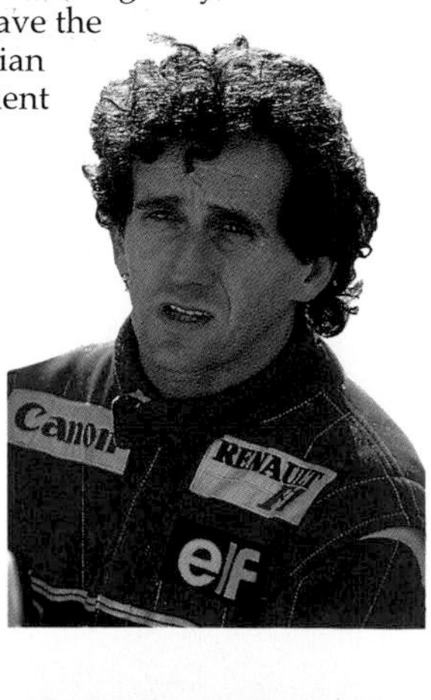
Canon
RENAULT
elf

PODIUM

The record for the greatest number of wins in one season is held jointly by two Renault drivers. By clinching nine Grand Prix victories in 1995, Michael Schumacher in fact equaled Nigel Mansell's record set in 1992 in a Williams-Renault; the previous record holder being Ayrton Senna with eight wins in a McLaren Honda.

Great Britain: 164 wins (27%) 16 drivers

Brazil: 79 wins (14%) 4 drivers

France: 78 wins (14%) 11 drivers

Austria: 40 wins (7%) 13 drivers

Italy: 39 wins (7%) 13 drivers

Argentina: 38 wins (7%) 3 drivers

Australia: 26 wins (5%) 2 drivers

US: 22 wins (4%) 5 drivers

Germany: 22 wins (4%) 3 drivers

Sweden: 12 wins (2%) 3 drivers

New Zealand: 12 wins (2%) 2 drivers

Belgium, South Africa, Switzerland, Canada, Mexico, Finland: 41 wins (7%) 8 drivers

WINS BY NATIONALITY

In terms of Grand Prix wins, Great Britain is Formula 1's most successful nation. Brazil, thanks to its three World Champions (Senna , Piquet, and Fittipaldi), is tied for second place with France, a country that owes two-thirds of its victories to just one man – Alain Prost. Italy, the second most prolific supplier of drivers to Grand Prix racing after Great Britain, ranks but fifth. Four countries have produced only one Grand Prix winner: Finland, Canada, South Africa, and Mexico.

YOUNGEST

Bruce McLaren became the youngest winner in F1's history by winning the 1959 US Grand Prix at the age of 22.

OLDEST

First past the flag in the 1951 French Grand Prix at the age of 53, Luigi Fagioli remains Formula 1's oldest-ever winner.

HAPPIEST

Taking the flag for the only F1 win of his career (Austria, 1975), Vittorio Brambilla lifted his arms in anticipation to show his joy. He promptly lost control of his car and smashed into the rails!

PERSEVERANCE

Andrea de Cesaris is without doubt F1's most persevering driver. From 208 starts, the Italian never won a race!

THE LUCKIEST

Peter Gethin headed Ronnie Peterson across the line of the 1971 Italian Grand Prix by just one hundredth of a second, the closest-ever finish recorded in Formula 1.

NUMBER OF WINS PER DRIVER

41 Senna (Braz.)
27 Stewart (GB)
24 Fangio (Arg.)
19 Schumacher (D)

51 Prost (F)
31 Mansell (GB)
25 Lauda (A)
Clark (GB)
23 Piquet (Braz.)
16 Moss (GB)

World Champions

THE FORMULA 1 WORLD CHAMPIONSHIP, motor racing's most coveted accolade, is awarded to the driver who scores the most points in the course of a season. Since 1950, 25 drivers have taken the crown. Some, like Fangio, have won it three, four, or five times. Certain drivers succeeded in clinching the title despite winning just one race in the course of the season, while Mansell was first past the flag nine times in his championship-winning year. The question regularly arises as to just who is the Champion of all Champions. While this debate is never likely to be definitively resolved, four drivers stand out in the history of Formula 1. They are, in order of appearance, Fangio, Clark, Prost, and Senna. Will we one day see Schumacher join the list?

JOCHEN RINDT
Jochen Rindt had promised his wife Nina that once he had won the world title, he would retire from Formula 1. Fate had it that he was killed at Monza in September 1970 and awarded the crown posthumously.

JOHN SURTEES
Six-times 500 cc motorbike Champion, John Surtees also won the world Formula 1 crown in 1964. His feat of taking the title on both two and four wheels – at the highest level possible – is unlikely to be repeated.

JIM CLARK
Perhaps the greatest of them all. Two world titles and 25 F1 wins barely do justice to his talent. He was killed in the prime of his career, aged 32, during a race of secondary importance one wet Sunday afternoon at Hockenheim.

AYRTON SENNA:
He is the only driver to have won three world titles before the age of 32. There is little doubt that Ayrton Senna would have gone on to pull level, and then pass, Prost and Fangio. Tragically, he lost his life at Imola on May 1, 1994 while leading the San Marino Grand Prix, a position we had become accustomed to seeing him in.

NUMBER OF CONSTRUCTOR'S TITLES SINCE 1958

Lotus, McLaren and Williams: 7

Ferrari : 8

Brabham and Cooper: 2

Benetton, Vanwall, BRM, Tyrrell, and Matra: 1

CONSTRUCTORS TO HAVE TAKEN A DRIVER TO THE TITLE SINCE 1950

Williams: 5

Lotus: 6

Ferrari and McLaren: 9

Brabham: 4

Benetton, Alfa Romeo, Mercedes *, Maserati*, Cooper, and Tyrrell: 2

BRM, and Matra: 1

* Fangio drove both a Mercedes and a Maserati on his way to winning the title in 1954.

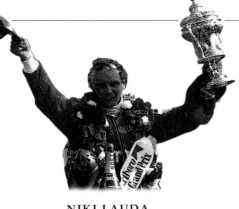

NIKI LAUDA
Niki Lauda "retired" twice from F1, the first time after a particularly close shave with death, the second because he was beginning to feel bored with the sport. On both occasions, he came back to add a further world title to his personal record.

CONSTRUCTORS' CHAMPIONSHIP
Since 1958, teams have had their own World Championship based on the combined points scored by its two drivers. The winning constructor is therefore not necessarily the team for which the champion driver races. The most recent example of this was in 1994 when Michael Schumacher took the Drivers' crown with Benetton-Ford while the Constructors' title went to Williams-Renault.

JUAN MANUEL FANGIO
Juan Manuel Fangio, who died in July 1995 at the age of 84, took five world titles during the eight years he raced in F1. During that time he raced in 51 Grands Prix and won 24 of them. What, one wonders, would he have achieved had his F1 career not started until the age of 38?

ALAIN PROST
His rivalry with Ayrton Senna set Formula 1 alight. Alain Prost retired from Grand Prix racing after winning his fourth title. His talent had in no way faded but, after 51 victories and 12 years spent at the peak of F1, the motivating spark had waned.

SCHUMACHER
Michael Schumacher took his first Grand Prix win at the age of 28 and was twice World Champion by the age of 26. Never before has a Formula 1 driver built up such an eloquent record so young. It remains to be seen whether his recent move to Ferrari will reap as much success as his years at Benetton.

WORLD F1 DRIVERS' CHAMPIONS (1950-1995)

Year	Driver	Constructor
1950	Farina (I)	Alfa Romeo
1951	Fangio (Arg.)	Alfa Romeo
1952	Ascari (I)	Ferrari
1953	Ascari (I)	Ferrari
1954	Fangio (Arg.)	Mercedes & Maserati
1955	Fangio (Arg.)	Mercedes
1956	Fangio (Arg.)	Lancia & Ferrari
1957	Fangio (Arg.)	Maserati
1958	Hawthorn (GB)	Ferrari
1959	Brabham (Aus.)	Cooper-Climax
1960	Brabham (Aus.)	Cooper-Climax
1961	P Hill (US)	Ferrari
1962	G Hill (GB)	BRM
1963	Clark (GB)	Lotus-Climax
1964	John Surtees (GB)	Ferrari
1965	Clark (GB)	Lotus-Climax
1966	Brabham (Aus.)	Brabham-Repco
1967	Hulme (NZ)	Brabham-Repco
1968	G Hill (GB)	Lotus-Ford
1969	Stewart (GB)	Matra-Ford
1970	Rindt (A)	Lotus-Ford
1971	Stewart (GB)	Tyrrell-Ford
1972	Fittipaldi (Braz.)	Lotus-Ford
1973	Stewart (GB)	Tyrrell-Ford
1974	Fittipaldi (Braz.)	McLaren-Ford
1975	Lauda (A)	Ferrari
1976	Hunt (GB)	McLaren-Ford
1977	Lauda (A)	Ferrari
1978	Andretti (US)	Lotus-Ford
1979	Scheckter (SA)	Ferrari
1980	Jones (Aus.)	Williams-Ford
1981	Piquet (Braz.)	Brabham-Ford
1982	Rosberg (Fin)	Williams-Ford
1983	Piquet (Braz.)	Brabham BMW
1984	Lauda (A)	McLaren-Porsche
1985	Prost (F)	McLaren-Porsche
1986	Prost (F)	McLaren-Porsche
1987	Piquet (Braz.)	Williams-Honda
1988	Senna (Braz.)	McLaren-Honda
1989	Prost (F)	Mclaren-Honda
1990	Senna (Braz.)	McLaren-Honda
1991	Senna (Braz.)	McLaren-Honda
1992	Mansell (GB)	Williams-Renault
1993	Prost (F)	Williams-Renault
1994	Schumacher (D)	Benetton-Ford
1995	Schumacher (D)	Benetton-Renault

On to the next race

THE RACE HAS FINISHED and the clamor of the engines has faded, but another race is already underway. This one is against the clock, for teams always like to have as much time as possible to prepare for the following Grand Prix. Drivers are the first to leave, some at the controls of personal planes. At the nearest international airport, another plane is preparing for an 8 o'clock takeoff with mechanics and engineers on board. Two hours after the checkered flag has dropped, the hurriedly loaded trucks finally get away. The aim is for personnel and equipment to be back at the factory on the Monday morning. Drivers have an extra day of rest at their disposal, since private testing never begins before the Tuesday.

São Paulo, Brazil:
10,000-km outward trip

Buenos Aires, Argentina:
2,000 km from São Paulo,
12,000 km back to Didcot

Imola, Italy:
2,800-km
return trip

Barcelona,
Spain:
3,000-km
return trip

Monte-Carlo,
Monaco:
2,400-km
return trip

Montreal, Canada:
12,000-km
return trip

Magny-Cours,
France:
1,400-km
return trip

Silverstone,
Great Britain:
140-km return trip

Hockenheim,
Germany:
2,000-km
return trip

A RACE AROUND THE WORLD
Transporter trucks make their way back to base as quickly as possible after the finish of a Grand Prix. The sooner they get back, the better the team is able to prepare for the following Grand Prix. On a European scale, Renault Sport's Viry-Châtillon premises in the Paris suburbs are more centrally located than the Williams factory in Didcot, which is some 100 km northwest of London. Silverstone, just 70 km from Didcot, is the Williams team's home Grand Prix. The farthest afield is Adelaide. Having left a month beforehand for the Japanese Grand Prix, cars return to the UK a week after the Australian round, having been shipped directly from Suzuka to the South Australian capital. This time, however, the work schedule is more relaxed, for Adelaide is the final Grand Prix of the season. The next world tour doesn't begin until after the winter break, in Melbourne, Australia.

THOROUGH CHECKUP
Cars return to the factory on the Monday or the Tuesday after a Grand Prix. This leaves mechanics just a few days – a week at most during the European "summer campaign" – to prepare for the following race. Before any revisions are made to the car's specification, a systematic six-point check is carried out.

STRIPPING THE CAR
Stripping the car takes half a day and allows mechanics to inspect parts and remove stones and rubber encrusted in the chassis.

ENGINE CHANGE
The first task awaiting mechanics when cars get back to the factory is to remove the engines from the chassis in order to ship them back to the engine supplier.

TRANSMISSION REVISION
Formula 1 transmissions are systematically rebuilt after every race. The bevel gears are inspected for wear while gears, shift-forks, and dog clutch are always changed.

Shock Absorbers: 500 km

Engine: 500 km

Transmission: 500 km

Wings: 500 km

Suspension parts: 3,000 km

Chassis: 6,000 km

LIFE EXPECTANCY
An estimated useful working life is established for each component on the car. As a precautionary measure, even if no sign of wear can be detected, parts are automatically replaced once this distance has been reached.

Adelaide, Australia: 14,000 km from Suzuka 20,000 km back to Didcot

Suzuka, Japan: 500 km from Aïda

Aïda, Japan: 14,000-km outward trip

Nürburgring, Germany: 2,400 km from Estoril 1,000 km back to Didcot

Estoril, Portugal: 2,600-km outward trip

Monza, Italy: 2,200-km return trip

Budapest, Hungary: 4,000-km return trip

Spa, Belgium : 700-km return trip

SEE YOU NEXT YEAR
Two hours after the winner has crossed the finish line, the circuit is practically empty. All that remain are the occasional scraps of litter, traces of rubber on the track, and a group of journalists busy finishing their articles in the press office. Drivers and spectators are all long gone as the last trucks, having loaded all their equipment, pull out of the paddock. There is always a tinge of sadness when the curtain falls on another Grand Prix. However, Formula 1 will be back in a year's time. Until then, the world tour continues, to other countries, to other circuits.

PARTS INSPECTION
Hubs and wishbones are coated with Ardrox, a red penetrating solution. This is cleaned off and a white solution is applied. If a red line appears, the part is cracked.

WHEEL-BEARING CHANGE
The wheel bearings, which are situated between the fixed stub axle and the rotating hub, are replaced after every race.

FRESH PAINT
Cars often come back with chipped paintwork caused by gravel thrown up during the race. They are repainted to ensure the smoothest possible flow of air across the body next time out.

Life after Formula 1

Alain Prost

D RIVERS VERY RARELY LEAVE FORMULA 1. In fact it's more often the other way round. Those that choose to pull out at the peak of their careers – like Hawthorn, Stewart, Hunt, Scheckter, Mansell, and Prost – tend to be exceptions. More frequently, with age, certain drivers begin by slipping down the grid before turning to alternative forms of motor racing. Indeed, some 60 ex-F1 drivers were racing in other types of competition in 1995. But what of those who stop altogether? About 20 or so have taken up TV commentary, while others have earned enough money from the sport to retire on their takings. Others move into totally new fields. Carlos Reutemann, for example, today governor of Argentina's Santa Fe province, is tipped by some as a future president of the South American republic.

ON THE OTHER SIDE OF THE CAMERA

About 20 F1 drivers still play an active role in today's F1 scene. Jackie Oliver manages the Arrows team, Jean-Pierre Jabouille is Team Director at Peugeot Sport, and Guy Edwards works as a sponsor hunter for Ligier. However, the majority of those still involved have taken up TV commentary, like Alain Prost (TFI), Derek Daly (ESPN), Jonathan Palmer (BBC), Jochen Mass (RTL), John Watson and Philippe Alliot (Eurosport), and Satoru Nakajima (Fuji TV). Not forgetting a special mention for the late James Hunt, who will long be remembered as a master of the art at the BBC.

Jackie Oliver

NUMBER OF GRAND PRIX
RACED BY TEAMS FOUNDED BY FORMER F1 DRIVERS

TEAM	GRANDS PRIX	DRIVER	YEAR
McLaren	427 *	Bruce McLaren (NZ)	Since 1966
Brabham	394	Jack Brabham (Aus)	1962–92
Ligier	310 *	Guy Ligier (F)	Since 1976
Arrows	272 *	Jackie Oliver (GB)	Since 1978
March	230	Alan Rees (GB)	1970–92
Larrousse	126*	Gérard Larrousse (F)	1987–94
Surtees	118	John Surtees (GB)	1970–78
Fittipaldi	104	Emerson Fittipaldi (Braz)	1975–82
Connaught	49	Kenneth McAlpine (GB)	1952–59
Penske	40	Roger Penske (US)	1974–77
Eagle	25	Dan Gurney (US)	1966–69
HWM	14	George Abecassis (GB)	1951–54
Hill	10	Graham Hill (GB)	1975
Merzario	10	Arturo Merzario (I)	1978–79
ERA	7	Leslie Johnson (GB)	1950–52
JBW	5	Brian Naylor (GB)	1959–61
LDS	5	Doug Serrurier (SA)	1962–68
Emeryson	4	Paul Emery (GB)	1956–62
LEC	3	David Purley (GB)	1977
Bellasi	2	Silvio Moser (CH)	1970–71
Alfa Special	2	Peter de Klerk (SA)	1963–65
Aston	2	Bill Aston (GB)	1952
Scarab	2	Lance Reventlow (US)	1960
Rebaque	1	Hector Rebaque (Mex)	1979
Amon	1	Chris Amon (NZ)	1974
Lyncar	1	John Nicholson (NZ)	1975

* TEAMS STILL INVOLVED IN FORMULA 1

TEAM MANAGERS

At one time, it wasn't rare for F1 drivers to start their own team, either during their career or at the end of it. Some, such as Brabham, McLaren, and Surtees, gave their names to their teams. Others, like Oliver (Arrows) or Gurney (Eagle), were somewhat less assertive. Except for Brabham and McLaren, few have tasted true success, a fact that supports those who claim that a driving career is not an open ticket to team management at a later date. Since Guy Ligier lost control of his team and Gérard Larrousse's recent withdrawal from the sport, Jackie Oliver is the sole driver-constructor still around today.

AT WHAT AGE DO DRIVERS LEAVE FORMULA 1?

Less than 30: 5

30 years: 6

31-32 years: 7

33-34 years: 8

35-36 years: 9

37-38 years: 10

39-40 years: 8

41-42 years: 6

43 or over: 4

AGE LIMIT

The average retirement age for drivers totaling more than 50 Grand Prix starts is 36. The grids are tending to get younger, however, and only three of the 1995 line-up were over 36: Berger, Moreno, and Brundle. But age isn't an insurmountable handicap. Nigel Mansell was 39 when he was crowned World Champion and the British driver took his last Grand Prix win at the age of 41. Clearly, the top drivers age well.

COLLECTOR
Phil Hill went back to California, where he restores vintage cars and pianos. He owns one of the most beautiful car museums in the US.

BUSINESSMAN
Nelson Piquet owns a number of Pirelli outlets in Brazil and tends to race less and less frequently, especially since his serious accident during the 1992 Indianapolis 500.

WHERE ARE THEY NOW?

MERCEDES W196
1954 World Champion (Fangio)
Mercedes Museum, Stuttgart

LOTUS 49
1968 World Champion (Hill)
Private collection (Setton), France

FERRARI 312 T2
1975 World Champion (Lauda)
Location unkown

BRABHAM BT52
1983 World Champion (Piquet)
Wheatcroft Museum, Donington

McLAREN MP4/5
1989 World Champion (Prost)
McLaren Collection, Woking

WILLIAMS FW14
1992 World Champion (Mansell)
Williams Collection, Didcot

Sports-Prototypes: 18 drivers – Mario Andretti, Baldi, Pescarolo, Bell, Grouillard, Acheson, etc.

Touring cars: 37 drivers – Jones, Rosberg, Laffite, Boutsen, Patrese, Alboreto, Warwick, Stuck, etc.

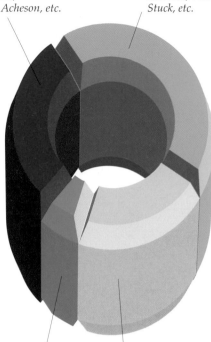

Miscellaneous: 5 drivers – Lammers, Schlesser, Berg, Byrne, Borgudd

Formula Indy: 13 drivers – Michael Andretti, Emerson and Christian Fittipaldi, Johansson, Fabi, Gugelmin, Cheever, Boesel, etc.

STILL RACING
Some 70 former Formula 1 stars still actively compete. The decline of Sports-Prototype racing has plugged one favorite area for reemployment, but the current return to favor of national touring car championships has provided new opportunities. Indy racing remains the favorite refuge for F1 stars, especially since it guarantees similar driving sensations to Grand Prix racing.

GOVERNOR
Carlos Reutemann, who once came very close to winning the world F1 title, is making a name for himself in politics. Elected governor of the Santa Fe Province in Argentina, he could well one day become president of his home country.

FARMER
Chris Amon, one of Formula 1's unlucky heroes, has returned to native New Zealand where he has followed on from his father, a wealthy landowner and sheep rancher.

AIRLINE PILOT
Niki Lauda has created his own airline company, Lauda Air. When his busy life leaves him the time, he likes nothing more than taking the controls of one of his Boeings.

INDY RACING
Emerson Fittipaldi, 1993 Indianapolis 500 winner, continues to compete in Indy racing. He also runs a chain of Hugo Boss shops and owns orange plantations in his native Brazil.

MANAGER
Keke Rosberg wears many hats. As well as driving for Opel in touring cars, he is a commentator for TV and looks after the F1 interests of fellow Finns Lehto and Hakkinen.

INDUSTRY
Jody Scheckter lives in Atlanta, where he has founded a company selling shooting simulators to the American army. Few of his professional contacts probably know that he is a former Formula 1 World Champion!

PUBLIC RELATIONS
Jackie Stewart works in public relations, notably for Ford. He also keeps an eye on the activities of his son Paul, who runs his own Formula 3000 team.

Index